MURDER & MYSTERY
ON THE
GREAT WESTERN RAILWAY

MIKE HOLGATE

HALSGROVE

First published in Great Britain in 2006

British Library Cataloguing-in-Publication Data
A CIP record for this title is available from the British Library

ISBN 1 84114 556 4
ISBN 978 1 84114 556 3

HALSGROVE

Halsgrove House
Lower Moor Way
Tiverton, Devon EX16 6SS
Tel: 01884 243242
Fax: 01884 243325
email: sales@halsgrove.com
website: www.halsgrove.com

Printed and bound by CPI Bath

CONTENTS

ACKNOWLEDGEMENTS

The author gratefully acknowledges the following organisations for their kind cooperation in providing newspaper articles and other information which made this book possible: Hammersmith & Fulham Archives & Local History Centre; Newton Abbot Reference Library; Plymouth Naval & Local Studies Library; Railway Studies Collection, Newton Abbot; Torquay Museum Society; Torquay Local Studies Library; West Country Studies Library, Exeter; Reading Local Studies Library.

ILLUSTRATIONS

Supplementing the author's own collection, the illustrations in this book were mainly obtained from the following antiquarian periodicals, books and guides: *Illustrated London News, Illustrated Police News, The Strand Magazine, Western Mail; Ward Lock's Pictorial and Descriptive Guide to Cornwall, 1907; The Great Western Railway Illustrated Guide c1875; The Blizzard in the West*, London, Simpkin, Marshall, Hamilton, Kent & Co., 1891; Burnard, Robert. *Dartmoor Pictorial Records*, 1891; Huish, Robert. *The Progress of Crime or the Authentic Memoirs of Maria Manning*, London,1849; MacDermot, E.T. *History of the Great Western Railway, Vol. 1 1833-1863*, London, Great Western Railway Company; 1927, MacDermot, E.T. *History of the Great Western Railway, Vol. 2 1863-1921*, London, Great Western Railway Company, 1931; Rhodes, A.J. *Dartmoor Prison*, London, John Lane The Bodley Head Ltd., 1933;

The author has taken the liberty of adapting or writing new captions for the *Punch* cartoons used on the title page of each chapter, which were obtained from *John Leech's Pictures of Life and Character*, London. Bradbury, Agnew & Co., 1887.

INTRODUCTION
Death on the Holiday Line

The Great Western Railway (GWR) successfully promoted itself as 'God's Wonderful Railway' and the glamorising of travel on smoky, grimy, hissing steam locomotives was no mean feat. This was partly achieved by the fact that the company primarily operated in the tourist playground of the West Country, transporting passengers from the capital to sunny resorts. During the Twentieth Century, the renowned 'Holiday Line', with self explanatory services like the Cornish Riviera and Torbay Express, gradually took over the mantle from what were initially Victorian business oriented services like 'The Flying Dutchman' (which originated from a racehorse of that name which won the Epsom Derby and the St Leger in 1849), and the 'Zulu' (inspired by the Anglo-Zulu war of 1879). For many years passengers from the lower orders were positively discouraged and high prices compelled them to travel like cattle in open-topped carriages tagged onto slow moving goods trains which dawdled in sidings and stopped at every tiny station. The GWR finally realised the full commercial possibilities of tourism when the 'Holiday Line' was officially launched in 1903.

Taking a quarter of a century to complete after the company received the Royal Assent in 1835, the line snaked it's way from London through Reading and Swindon to Bristol – 'The Gateway to the West', before passing via Bath and Taunton in Somerset then Exeter and Plymouth in Devon to the Royal Albert Bridge – 'The Gateway to Cornwall' which completed the route from Paddington to Penzance shortly before the death of its creator Isambard Kingdom Brunel in 1859.

7

FAREWELL LAMENT TO THE BROAD GAUGE
Pater (reading paper): 'They say the broad gauge is dead'
Mater: 'Where will one find room in those ghastly narrow carriages?'

Because of the number of railroad companies initially involved, the wayward route from London to Penzance humorously dubbed the 'Great Way Round' was described by poet Horatio Brown in the following extract from A *Farewell Lament to the Broad Gauge* published in 1891:

Triumphant pride of him who drives
From Paddington to far St Ives.
Drive on! And driving let me know
The golden West, it's warmth, it's glow
Pass Thames with all his winding maze;
Sweet Clifton dreaming in a haze;
And farther yet, past Taunton Vale;
And Dawlish rocks, and Teignmouth sail,
And Totnes, where the dancing Dart
Comes seaward with a gladsome heart;
Then let me feel the wind blow free
From levels of the Cornish sea.
Ah! Western lad, would I might be
A partner in that ecstasy.

The GWR was justly proud of its safety record, although its most distinguished passenger Queen Victoria was always apprehensive and insisted on travelling at a maximum speed of 40mph. These wishes were politely ignored for years until the monarch made her final and slowest-ever journey – on her funeral train. Incidents of violent crime on the GWR line were exceedingly rare although the company was perhaps fortunate that it abandoned its interest in the Metropolitan Railway in 1863; for a quarter of a century later 'Jack the Ripper' went on the rampage and one marvellous theory suggests that the atrocities were committed by a railway employee who committed the dastardly deeds before escaping from the scene of the crime via the nearest access to the Underground.

However, in stark contrast to the 'Romance of the GWR', promoting an image of cheery passengers and staff, there were inevitably dramatic casualties of the railroad; assembled within this volume is a collection of tragic stories involving murder, suicide and misadventure. Broadly covering the golden age of steam – the 100 year period between the GWR's appointment of genius Isambard Kingdom Brunel in 1833 and the death of eminent locomotive engineer George Jackson Churchward in 1933, it is fitting that this work begins with an account of the accident-prone life of the former and concludes with the ironic death on the railway of the latter, particularly as 9th April 2006 marked the 200th anniversary of the birth of Brunel and 31st January 2007, the 150th anniversary of the birth of Churchward.

Mike Holgate
March 2006

STEAMY TALES
'Sir, please remember
where we are; this is
the Great Western
Railway!'

9

THE ROMANCE AND DRAMA OF THE GREAT WESTERN RAILWAY

Two contrasting views of the scenic, yet, dangerous stretch of the line between Dawlish and Teignmouth originally constructed for the South Devon Railway by Isambard Kingdom Brunel. Above (1850): A broad gauge train passes visitors strolling in the sunshine along the beach near the tunnel adjacent to the seaward rock formation called the Parson and the Clerk. Below (1855): Passengers precariously leave their stranded train and scramble over rocks to negotiate the storm-damaged seawall before boarding the waiting connection to complete their journey to Exeter.

THE RACE AGAINST TIME
Old Father Time: 'Make way! Make way!'
Equine Lover: 'I say, don't frighten the horses'

1

The Accident-Prone Life
of Isambard Kingdom Brunel

God created Man and a great man created 'God's Wonderful Railway'. Precocious twenty-six-year-old Isambard Kingdom Brunel was appointed engineer of the newly formed Great Western Railway Company in 1833, and two years later, when the company was incorporated by an Act of Parliament, he congratulated himself with a note in his diary declaring, 'I am thus engineer to the finest work in England'. This optimism was expressed about a railway that did not yet exist but thanks largely to the vision and brilliance of the country's greatest engineer, the GWR remains the best-loved name from the age of steam.

Brunel could certainly not be accused of playing safe by sticking to established practice during his career, boldly adopting the broad gauge track of 7' 0¼" (2.14m) in preference to the narrow gauge 4' 8½" (1.43m) and experimenting with the more efficient, environmentally friendly Atmospheric Engine as an alternative to locomotives. In retrospect these may appear to have been glorious failures but he dared to be different. Nor did he content himself with solving the enormous problems of route, gradients, tunnels, bridges, plus the design of station buildings incum-

bent in the task of developing a railroad stretching from the Capital to Cornwall; for no
sooner had Parliament given the 'signal' for
the first line of communication between
London and Bristol in 1835 than he turned
his attention to a plan to connect Bristol
with New York by designing a series of
revolutionary steamships.

The 'Little Giant' obviously underesti-
mated the toll on his health that his heavy
workload would induce. His early demise was
undoubtedly accelerated by the extra demands
on his time, which resulted from the burdens
of unexpected complications, and unfortunate accidents, which regularly occurred to

*Isambard Kingdom Brunel
– The Little Giant*

blight the progress of his projects. In fact, it was such an incident, which
inadvertently gave him the opportunity to build the GWR. In January
1828, he was assisting his father; eminent engineer Marc Brunel, to build
the first tunnel under the River Thames when timber supports collapsed
and a torrent of water flooded the chamber killing sixteen workmen.
Young Brunel was seriously injured by a falling beam and was narrowly
rescued from drowning when a search party found him floating in the
water unconscious. Having sustained severe internal injuries he journeyed to Bristol for a long convalescence where his boredom was eased
by the announcement that a competition was to be held to design a bridge
to span Clifton Gorge. The adjudicator was that doyen of bridge builders
Thomas Telford and Brunel's design was selected, although work on the
project was later abandoned due to lack of funds. Nevertheless, Brunel's
potential was recognised by city merchants who had sponsored the
bridge competition and ensured that he was considered when they
sought to engage a civil engineer to construct a railroad from Bristol to
London. His appointment to the newly formed GWR company in March
1833, awarded after submitting a masterpiece of surveying for the pro-
posed line from to Paddington to Bristol Meads, was the first strand of a
railway network which threaded through the South West, encompassing
the Bristol and Exeter Railway, the South Devon Railway, the West
Cornwall Railway and the Cornwall Railway. The GWR invested in all of
these companies and eventually took them over completely, doubtless
sharing the belief entered in Brunel's journal, 'it's a proud thing to
monopolise the west as I do'.

Brunel struggled to complete the construction of the railroad from

Paddington to Penzance throughout the remaining twenty-six years of his life. The ponderous progress of the GWR involved not only surmounting numerous complex engineering problems, for much of Brunel's time was consumed by attending meetings trying to persuade owners to part with their land, potential shareholders to part with their money, company directors to accept his projections and parliamentary committees to accept his proposals. The actual construction of the railroad was also fraught with difficulty, disappointment, delays and danger. During surveys and construction of the line, Brunel supervised work by travelling in a black horse-drawn carriage of his own design, stocked with plans, engineering instruments and a plentiful supply of his trademark cigars. With more than a hint of black humour, in view of his periodic brushes with death, the carriage was irreverently nicknamed the 'Flying Hearse'.

The first section of the GWR opened between Paddington and Maidenhead at the beginning of June 1838, but Brunel nearly did not survive to see it. On the last day of March, he had an accident on board his newly built paddle steamer SS *Great Western*. He was helping with preparations for her maiden voyage to New York when a serious fire broke out in the boiler room. Descending a ladder to inspect the damage, a badly burnt rung gave way and Brunel plummeted eighteen feet, until his fall was broken when he landed on the captain of the vessel, who was using a hosepipe to douse the flames. Peering through the clouds of belching black smoke, the skipper saw the body of the ship's designer lying in deep water, which had accumulated, from the pumps and fire-hoses. To save the unconscious engineer from drowning, a rope was lowered and he was hauled to safety. The ship ran aground on Canvey Island where Brunel was taken ashore and spent many weeks recuperating from his injuries. The damage to the SS *Great Western* was quickly repaired and the vessel was awarded the cherished Blue Riband when she completed a momentous voyage across the Atlantic in record time. The triumphant return of the vessel to her homeport was greeted by cheering crowds. The *Bristol Mirror* observed the historic significance of Brunel's achievement: 'The joy and pleasure announced by all classes has been unequalled in the city for many years, and they almost stand level with the tidings from the Nile, Trafalgar Bay, and the plains of Waterloo'.

The following year, Brunel had another near death experience in an accident on his own railroad. Late in the afternoon on Thursday 13 June 1839, Brunel, accompanied by the superintendent of the locomotive department, Seymour Clarke, went for a trial run on the engine *Hurricane* pulling three empty carriages. Brunel and Clarke rode on the tender with

The Hurricane *was taken out for a trial run from the Engine House at Paddington*

the intention of travelling from Paddington as far as the new terminal at Twyford, then, when a mechanical problem occurred, decided to curtail their journey and return. They began reversing back along the track oblivious to the fact that the locomotive *Thunder* was on the same line getting up steam in readiness to haul the 5pm train from Paddington. The Grim Reaper beckoned when both engines were smashed in the inevitable collision that occurred adjacent to Kensal Green cemetery. The stationary *Thunder* was derailed and the carriages on the *Hurricane* were completely destroyed as they cushioned the blow for the occupants of the engine. Messrs Brunel and Clarke were badly shaken but escaped with nothing more serious than badly bruised egos.

Brunel often worked around the clock and could rarely spare the time to observe the Sabbath. Therefore, at 5am on Sunday 25 October 1840, he was on the spot to witness a fatal railway accident as he was waiting for a train to Paddington at the temporary terminus at Farringdon Road Station. He was surprised to see a baggage train hauled by the engine *Fire King* run right through the station and collide with a goods truck in the carriage shed before crashing through the doors of the building and ploughing into an adjoining field. Four passengers were injured and the driver John Ross and guard James Marlow were killed. Brunel was called to give evidence at the inquest held at the nearby Railway Tavern where his testimony confirmed that the accident had been caused solely by the driver neglecting to turn off the steam. The fireman Jim James was thrown clear and did not see what had happened in the cab as he was on the tender gathering coke for the boiler at the time of the accident. He had noticed nothing unusual in the driver's behaviour and therefore, it was surmised that John Ross had either fallen asleep or suddenly been taken ill at the controls. Brunel had observed the driver standing motionless as the engine passed him. The unfortunate victim had pitched head first between the tender and cab causing him to be decapitated when the engine reared up in the crash. The jury absolved the railway company of any blame and recorded a verdict of 'Accidental death'.

The GWR suffered their first full-blown railway disaster early in the morning on Friday 24 December 1841, when a goods train, consisting of the locomotive *Hecla*, two third class carriages carrying thirty-eight passengers, and seventeen goods wagons loaded with eight hundred barrels of oysters and baskets of fish, was buried in a landslide which had covered the track to a depth of four feet at Sonning Cutting, midway between Maidenhead and Reading. When the engine ran into the mound of earth, the heavily laden goods wagons shunted and crushed the open-topped carriages against the tender inflicting terrible injuries on the packed occupants. The driver and fireman leapt off the engine when they spotted the obstacle in their path but there was no escape for the passengers and nine men lost their lives. A *Times* reporter described the harrowing scene: 'The cries of the maimed and wounded, and the shrieks of the dying, at this moment, it was impossible to describe. It was at once a scene of destruction and horror of the most lamentable and heartrending character'.

Brunel travelled to the scene on a work train taking one hundred navvies to clear the obstruction, and then investigated the tragedy. Coroner, Mr May, conducted an inquest held near the scene of the accident at the Shepherd's House Inn. Called as an expert witness Brunel gave an invaluable insight into how deeply involved he was in every aspect of the day-to-day management of the railway: 'In this particular instance of the Sonning Cutting I saw a small slip about three weeks ago. As I observed that it was only a superficial slip, I did not consider there

Sonning Cutting: The scene of the GWR's first railway disaster

was any danger to be apprehended. I have passed many times since and not observed any change. On Friday morning, I arrived at the spot a few hours after the accident, when I examined the slip, which had then taken place. It was a totally distinct slip. ... The disturbed ground of the new slip touched the old slip; but the slips themselves started in different parts of the slope, and in different strata. ... As there have been discussions here and in the public papers relative to the position of the passenger tenders, perhaps I may be allowed to mention that the reason for putting the passenger trucks next to the engine arises from the danger to which a luggage train is considered most liable – namely, its being overtaken by another train, in consequence of its being much slower, and unavoidably less punctual than passenger trains. Also, the danger arising from the breaking of axles is greater in the luggage trains from the great weight. In either case the front of the train is the best position for passenger trucks. The passenger truck was put in the middle of the train on Friday night by my order ... I thought it would have been better not to send down any luggage train that night; but there were so many applications for places, being Christmas Eve ... Our feelings and interests are, of course involved in providing the best place possible for passengers, and, upon the whole, it is my decided opinion, that near the engine is preferable to behind the goods trucks. Many accidents might arise to passengers, if placed at the rear of luggage trains'.

After a deliberation of two hours the inquest jury recorded a verdict of 'accidental death' on the deceased, the majority of whom were stone masons who had been working on a temple in London and were on their way home to spend the festive season with their families in Gloucester. In addition, the jury levied a charge, called a deodand, of £1000 against the GWR, whom they believed had caused the accident by placing the carriages behind the tender and not adequately monitoring the cutting when they were aware there was a problem. In a report to the Board of Trade, Sir Frederick Smith attributed the landslip to excessive rainfall and having inspected the correct angle of the embankment absolved Brunel from blame: 'I do not imagine that any engineer would have thought it necessary to give the sides of this cutting a greater slope than two to one, and therefore there has been, in my opinion, no error in the construction'.

Due to the accident at Sonning, Brunel spent little time with his family that Christmas. This was not an unusual situation, in a letter to a friend he wrote that his workload allowed him little time for relaxation, 'I am rarely much under twenty hours a day at it'. On one of the rare occasions he spent time playing with his children, it almost cost him his life. He was showing them a trick – placing a half-sovereign in his mouth and pretending to recover it from his ear, when he accidentally swallowed the coin which lodged in his windpipe. With his life in danger, regular press bulletins reported on the perilous attempts to extricate the object. The saga continued for six weeks during April and May in 1843. A tracheotomy failed to clear the obstruction before Brunel solved the problem himself by observing the action of a full-length swinging mirror. Having designed an apparatus on this principle he was strapped to it then inverted before a surgeon slapped him repeatedly on the back causing a fit of coughing which expelled the foreign body from his throat. The nation breathed a sigh of relief when the newspaper headlines announced 'It's Out!'

After a period of convalescence Brunel's next escape from death was on more familiar territory and occurred on Tuesday 17 June 1845, when the recently introduced express service from London to Exeter, covering the 200 mile journey 'in the incredibly short space of four hours and a half' was derailed between West Drayton and Slough at Dog Kennels Bridge. The train, consisting of four carriages and a luggage van, suddenly

Brunel escaped unscathed from a railway accident near West Drayton

oscillated violently as the luggage van came off the rails, causing the carriages to break away from the tender before rolling off the tracks and down an embankment. The passengers were hurled from their seats and enveloped in clouds of dust. Miraculously, although forty people sustained injuries there were no fatalities. Walking away virtually unscathed from a train wreck for the second time were Isambard Kingdom Brunel and Seymour Clarke. They were among the 150 passengers on the train and escaped unharmed having suffered only 'trifling bruises'. In an interview with the press, Clarke explained what had happened: 'The cause of the accident appears to have been that the luggage van, which was a four-wheeled vehicle and the lightest in the train, was, for some cause which cannot at present be ascertained, thrown off the line; the engine and the other carriages remaining in their proper positions on the rails. It proceeded thus until it came to the cast-iron girders or troughs of a bridge thrown over a road leading from Langley to Iver, when it seems that it struck one of these girders, which threw it off the timbers into the ballast of the line, pulling with it, and against the iron girders, the remainder of the train'.

Daniel Gooch, appointed GWR locomotive engineer at the age of twenty-one, identified the greatest fault of the company's chief engineer. 'One feature of Mr Brunel's character (and it is one that gave him a great deal of extra and unnecessary work) was, he fancied no one could do anything but himself … '. A consequence of this inability to delegate responsibility to assistants employed to supervise his projects resulted in Brunel being the greatest user of the railway, crisscrossing the country to check on work in progress. It was while returning from one of these journeys that he came upon the scene of an accident at Wootton Bassett. A 'cheap excursion train' was returning to Bristol packed with trippers who had spent a day in the Capital. Leaving Paddington on the evening of Friday 20 September 1850, it reached Swindon at 11.15pm, then just after passing Wootton Bassett, collided with an empty horsebox, which had rolled out of a siding onto the track. The engine and the first four carriages ran off the track and down an embankment into a field. The driver and fireman were flung clear of their wrecked engine and rushed to assist their passengers. Fortunately, although many broken bones were sustained, there were no fatalities. The first carriage had landed on its side and the occupants were released by smashing through the roof with a sledgehammer. The Bristol to London mail train arrived upon the scene of devastation carrying Brunel who aided the sufferers.

The GWR engineer also initiated an investigation to solve the mystery of how the horsebox had found its way onto the track. It was suspected that the horsebox had been deliberately set in motion by a passer-by, but the only action taken was the arrest of a railway policeman William

Bristol Temple Meads

White. He was charged with neglect of duty and appeared before the magistrates three days later at the Goddard Arms. The horsebox had been placed in the siding using 'scotches' – wooden wedges placed behind the wheels, and it was then one of a policeman's many and varied tasks to ensure it remained safely secured. Unfortunately for the accused, travelling in the first carriage of the derailed train was the distinctly unimpressed head of the GWR police at Bristol, Superintendent Richard Burton, who gave his version of events to the court: 'We had passed the station only a short time when we came into collision with something. I sang out to the people to keep their seats, and the words were hardly out of my mouth before we went down the bank and turned over in a ditch at the bottom. The second carriage turned over also. When I got out I said to White, "How did this occur?" He replied, "I don't know, indeed". I asked him if he had seen the horsebox in the siding. He said he had. I asked him if it was properly secured. He replied that Skull told him it was all right when he relieved him. Skull was the day policeman. I said, "That is nothing to you, you should have satisfied yourself it was all right". His answer was, "Well sir, I ought to have done so". I asked him if he had gone himself and examined whether the horsebox was scotched or not. He said, "No, I did not"'.

William White, a policeman with eight years service said in his defence: 'On Friday night I relieved the day policeman, who told me before leaving that everything was all right. I did not go and see if the horsebox was properly scotched but could see it was all right and not on the main line. Another reason I did not go down was that there were many goods of value on the station platform; if any of them had been stolen I would have had to pay for them, or been dismissed, or perhaps both. I also had responsibility for the signal lamp in the middle of a public crossing, and any person passing might turn on the red light resulting in the stoppage of a train. If I had gone down to inspect the scotches my back would have been towards the signal and I could not see whether the signal had been meddled with. Several times during the evening I observed that the horsebox was standing in its proper place, although I cannot say that the scotches were under the wheels'.

The Magistrates did not accept these excuses and found that the charge of neglect of duty had been proved. In their view the testimony of the accused himself confirmed that he had not complied with procedures, which involved the safety of people's lives. They concluded that the consequences in this case had been serious – though providentially not fatal; therefore, the sentence of the court was that William White should serve two calendar months imprisonment.

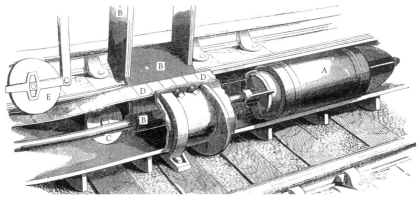

A section of the atmospheric tube showing (a) the piston
(b) the link to the piston carriage (c) a wheel that raises the sliding valve
(d) and (e) a wheel that closes the sliding valve

Brunel's maritime ventures continued with the design of the SS *Great Britain*, the first propeller-driven, steam powered iron ship to regularly cross the Atlantic. The strength of the vessel was severely tested when it struck rocks and ran aground with one hundred and eighty passengers on board off the coast of Ireland in September 1846. This incident forced the Great Western Steamship Company to go into liquidation. The company's demise was hastened when Brunel had to postpone plans to inspect the damage to the ship, the reason being that he was confronted with insoluble problems resulting from his decision to install an experimental system on the South Devon Railway, an episode that became notorious as the 'Atmospheric Caper'.

The South Devon Railway running from Exeter to Plymouth, with a branch line from Newton Abbot to Torquay, passed along the banks of the River Exe and skirted the hilly southern edge of Dartmoor. Brunel persuaded the directors of the company to adopt a revolutionary system whereby air pressure pumped from a stationary engine replaced conventional locomotive power. Engine houses were built at three-mile intervals along the track at Exeter, Countess Weir, Turf, Starcross, Dawlish, Teignmouth, Summer House, Newton Abbot, Dainton, Totnes and Torquay. These were designed to pump air through tubes placed between the tracks that propelled the train when linked to the leading 'piston carriage'. The driver increased or reduced the speed of the train by operating a mechanism that opened or closed a sliding leather valve thereby controlling the flow of air behind a piston running along the tube. The smoke-free, noiseless, smooth running trains impressed passengers when trials took place between Exeter and Teignmouth. However, the system was to prove unreliable. The pumping stations frequently broke down and the new technology could be dangerous for workers. In May 1848, an operative on the air pump at Exeter, was injured when a valve fell and crushed his foot resulting in the amputation of his leg at the Royal Devon & Exeter Hospital. Within a month of this accident, two 'greasers', employed to smear lubricant on the leather valve and keep it supple, were both killed in separate incidents when they failed to notice the approach of a silent train. Sealing compound was also continually applied to the tube to prevent air escaping from the valves and joints – a problem which highlights the great disadvantage of the system – for when the vacuum failed, all traffic was brought to a halt. Conversely, if the leather valve stuck and the piston remained in the tube, stopping was impossible. In this situation trains ran right through the station leaving waiting passengers stranded on the platform, while those wishing to alight were forced to journey to the next designated stop.

Despite the designer's assertion that it would 'cost too much money to fail', the railroad dubbed locally as 'Brunel's plaything, the unmanageable atmospheric', was abandoned after two years of stop-start operating, resulting in a catastrophic financial loss to the company's shareholders. They also had to bear the cost of recurring landslips from sandstone cliffs and breaches to the dry stone seawall along the storm lashed section of track by Parson's Tunnel between Dawlish and Teignmouth. In October 1846, the directors pledged to 'spare no effort or expense' to solve the problem when the combination of a high tide and south-easterly gale virtually destroyed the wall. Alarmingly, it was breached at eight points and gaps opened measuring up to one hundred yards in length. Third class passengers seated in open trucks were used to running the gauntlet of the sea and being drenched by waves at high tide, but now first and second class passengers also suffered inconvenience when they were compelled to alight from the train and clamber over rocks to avoid the rubble strewn flooded track and board another train waiting at the other side of the obstacle. *Woolmer's Exeter and Plymouth Gazette* criticised the railroad's coastal location, 'Were it not a life and death affair to public and shareholders, the scene is very grand … as a main trunk line from London to the Land's End it is utterly preposterous, and is now so considered to be by every man between those termini'.

Brunel was quickly onsite and confidently assured everyone that he could overcome the problem of the sea, although he was contradicted by Stephen Matterface, a local 'character' from Dawlish, who prophesised within earshot of the engineer: 'This is Neptune's youngest son: next time he will send his eldest; if that will not do, next time he will come himself,

A major landslip on the South Devon Railway 1853

and sweep them all away'. 'Old Stephen' was almost proved right; Neptune's 'eldest son' did his worst throughout January and February 1853, when bad weather and high seas caused four cliff falls. Sandstone disturbed by previous blasting poured down and blocked the track, severely disrupting services, although luckily, all the slips occurred when there were no trains passing for, as the *Times* commented, 'had that been the case, there must have been an immense destruction of human life, as thousands of tons of rock have been precipitated over the line'. 'Neptune' emerged to inflict further destruction on Friday 16 February 1855. Rough seas pounded the seawall causing the structure to bulge alarmingly. Precautionary measures taken by workmen to avert impending disaster failed as a terrific south-westerly gale and a spring tide at its height crashed through the wall ripping up railway track and telegraph poles that were washed into the sea. However, the prediction of 'Old Stephen' and the rage of 'Neptune' were denied by Brunel's improvements, which limited the damage to a fifty-foot section inflicted during the worst imaginable ravages of nature. The *Torquay Chronicle and General Directory* asserted: 'It is right to state that the wall was well built, and has been declared by a practical man to be one the best pieces of masonry in the country, but the late gale having cleared the whole of the sand from the beach; the foundation became exposed, and it was then discovered that the red rock on which the sea wall was built had been completely fretted away by the friction of the sand and water'.

Four years after his victory over 'Neptune', Brunel was terminally ill with a kidney complaint and too sick to attend the grand opening of his acclaimed Royal Albert Bridge straddling the River Tamar – the final obstacle in his dream to complete a railroad from Paddington to Penzance. Without fanfare he later viewed the work by travelling slowly across the bridge lying on a specially prepared flat truck. Brunel had finally laid the nightmare of a recurring ghost which he wrote about to a friend shortly after the opening of his first railroad at Paddington almost a quarter of a century earlier: 'If ever I go mad, I shall have the Ghost of the Opening of the Railway … standing in front of me, holding out its hand, and when it steps forward, a little swarm of devils in the shape of leaky pick-tanks, uncut timber, half-finished station-houses, sinking embankments, broken screws, absent gauge-plates, unfinished drawings and sketches will, quietly and quite as a matter of course and as I ought to have expected it, lift up my ghost and put him a little further off than before'.

Brunel had built his last railway and it might have been kinder if he had died immediately after his conquest of the Tamar, but he survived for another four months, stubbornly clinging to life, in the hope that he would see a successful conclusion to probably his most stressful project, the launching of what was then the largest ship afloat – SS *Great Eastern*. Boarding the ship berthed on the River Thames on 5 September, Brunel was seized by a stroke. He had recovered from minor forms of this condition twice before when struck down in 1842 and 1845, but this third attack was far more serious. Paralysed but conscious he was cared for at his London home in Duke Street, while his leviathan made ready for her maiden voyage. He lingered between life and death for a further ten days hoping for good news – but when the news came it was devastating. Sailing from Weymouth, the gigantic steam ship was severely damaged by a tremendous explosion in her boiler room, resulting in the death of five stokers. Informed of this tragedy, Brunel finally lost the will to live. Having survived three strokes, two railway accidents, two narrow escapes from drowning and a life-threatening object lodged in his throat, he finally succumbed at the ninth time of asking. With typical thoroughness, he was laid to rest in a vault he had designed himself at Kensal Green cemetery – near the scene of his first railway accident.

Daniel Gooch paid this personal tribute to Brunel in his diary: 'On the 15th September I lost my oldest and best friend. … By his death the greatest of England's engineers was lost, the man of the greatest originality of thought and power of execution, bold in his plans but right. The commercial world thought him extravagant, but although he was so, great things are not done by those who sit down and count the cost of every thought and act. He was a true and sincere friend, a man of the highest honour, and his loss was deplored by all who had the pleasure to know him'.

Gooch later salvaged Brunel's reputation as a shipbuilder when he bought the *Great Eastern* for a fraction of its cost so that 'the world may still be thankful to my old friend Brunel that he designed and carried out the construction of so noble a work'. The decision was vindicated when the vessel was utilised to lay the first telegraph cable across the Atlantic in June 1866. In Bristol, where Brunel's name was revered, his design for the Clifton Suspension Bridge was resurrected and built as a lasting memorial. Opened with great pomp and ceremony on 8 December 1864, the structure was compared favourably with the best of the engineer's railway works in the West of England. These achievements include the two-mile long Box Tunnel between Bath and Swindon, the stone viaduct at Chippenham and the tubular iron bridge at Saltash. The triumphant and tortuous life of an engineering genius, which, although charmed, still ended prematurely at the age of fifty-three was summarised by a phase in his obituary that appeared in the *Times*: 'Great was the glory, but greater was the strife'.

A *tribute to Brunel from the* Illustrated London News

TROUBLE AT THE BORDER
Young Lady: 'Oh dear, I've forgotten my passport'
Guard: 'Don't worry Miss, you won't need one on the Cornish Riviera'

2

The Cornish Viaduct Tragedies

As preparations were being made for the historic opening of the rail link between Devon and Cornwall, made possible by the construction of one of Brunel's greatest works the Royal Albert Bridge, its designer was attempting to improve his rapidly failing health holidaying on the Continent. Therefore, he was absent from the ceremony on Monday 2 May 1859 – as were the majority of the directors of the Cornwall Railway Company whose special train hauled by the engine *Argo* embarrassingly broke down between Truro and Saltash. The officials arrived too late to hear an address presented at noon to Prince Albert, in which the Mayor of Saltash proudly declared that the Royal Albert Bridge was 'a work destined in our opinion to be a memento to generations yet unborn of your Royal Highness's name and memory, as also of the skill and perseverance evinced by the eminent engineer in the construction thereof '.

The South Devon Railway from Exeter to Plymouth now met the new Cornwall Railway at Millbay that crossed the River Tamar and ran to Truro where it joined the West Cornwall Railway, which had opened at Penzance in 1852.

A broadsheet ballad celebrated the completion of the railroad, which

The opening of the Royal Albert Bridge at Saltash

would soon make it possible to travel along Brunel's broad gauge track from the Capital to Cornwall:

From Saltash to St Germans, Liskeard and St Austell,
The County of Cornwall was all in a bustle,
Prince Albert is coming the people did say
To open the Bridge and the Cornwall railway.
From Redruth and Camborne, St Just in the west
The people did flock all dressed in their best.
From all parts of England you'll now have a chance
To travel by steam right down to Penzance.

Prince Albert enjoyed a short journey on the Cornwall Railway travelling from Saltash to inspect Coombe Viaduct – one of forty-three covering the difficult terrain over a distance of eighty miles from Plymouth to Penzance. Designed by Brunel and constructed from timber these structures were a staggering achievement. The viaducts were also to become the scene of many tragedies, the first of which occurred only four days after the official opening of the Cornwall Railway.

On Friday 6 May 1859, the 7.25pm train left Plymouth four minutes late with about forty passengers bound for Truro. Behind the engine a first class carriage was sandwiched between two second class carriages with a luggage van bringing up the rear. The train had made up the lost time as it approached Grove Viaduct crossing a small inlet of the River Lynher. As it descended down a slight incline to the viaduct at a speed of 30mph, there was a peculiar jolting motion as part of the train came off the tracks. Richard Padden, the guard travelling in the last second class carriage, which contained half the passengers, applied the hand brake with full force and successfully brought the carriage and the luggage van behind to a standstill on the viaduct. Looking out of the window he saw that the engine and the first two carriages had plunged off the parapet into the lake thirty feet below. Getting out he examined his carriage and found that he had applied the brake with so much pressure that the coupling chains had snapped, otherwise the whole train would have gone over the viaduct. He also observed that the front wheels of the carriage and the hind wheels of the luggage van were off the rails. Scrambling down the bank Padden saw the other carriages immersed in seven feet of water. Bravely, he swam out to rescue passengers who fortunately all escaped with nothing more than cuts and bruises. Joined by waterman, Henry Spencer, who had run to the spot after witnessing the accident, the pair tried in vain to save the lives of the head guard and engine crew. Guard William Hoskins, travelling in the second class carriage behind the engine, had been killed outright by a blow to the head when the first class carriage crashed through the roof of the guard's compartment. The engine was lying upside down below the water buried in deep mud that had suffocated driver Henry Briscombe and fireman David Hannaford. Labourers were brought to dig out the bodies submerged beneath the engine. The engine driver was found lying on his back with his arms out-stretched whilst the stoker was lying face down with his hands by his

The runaway train passed St Michael's Mount

head. At an inquest held on the casualties at St Germans, Brunel's chief engineer Mr Brereton was called to account but could provide no explanation for the fatal accident. At the direction of the Coroner, Mr Jago, the jury recorded a verdict of 'Accidental death' with a recommendation that when travelling down an incline the speed of trains should be reduced especially where the line was new.

On a lighter note, on Tuesday 3 April 1860, a runaway train 'escaped' from the terminus at Penzance and after passing St Michael's Mount with a posse of railwaymen in hot pursuit made it across the viaduct at Chyandour before being recaptured at Carn Brae. The flight occurred at 5am shortly after the engine's boiler had been fired up in readiness for the driver and fireman to take the train into service. The preparation took place in the sheds before the workman responsible alighted from the engine to attend to other duties. When he returned the loco was gone. He had carelessly left the regulator open and the brake off, so when the steam rose to the required temperature away went the riderless 'puffer' for a jaunt on the main line. After crossing Chyandour Viaduct, it passed through Marazion Station, crawled slowly up a steep incline before reaching the crest of the hill and descending rapidly at a speed of 60mph through St Ives, Hayle, Gwinear and Camborne. By this time it had smashed its way through several gates at level crossings and wooden souvenirs were borne along on the cowcatcher. After a run of seventeen miles, the fire began to burn out and the breathless engine gradually slowed allowing a railwayman to jump aboard and bring the fugitive to

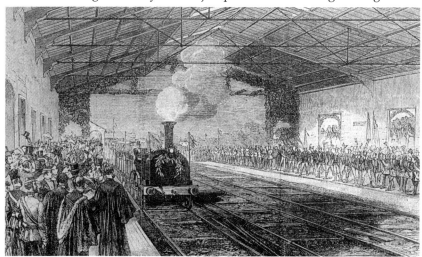

The opening of the branch line at Falmouth

a halt. Luckily, apart from the wreckage left in its wake no harm had been done by the runaway. It was indeed fortunate that it did not meet another train on the single track crossing the viaduct.

Following Brunel's death, another eight viaducts based on his designs were incorporated on the Truro to Falmouth branch line, which opened in 1863. Within months of opening, a fatal accident occurred to Charles Rillstone, a printer from Helston, who regularly commuted between two employers, one at Truro and the other at Penryn. It was his habit on the 'up' journeys to travel as far as Perran Station and then walk to Truro. These tiring journeys were to lead to his death on Thursday 28 January 1864. Purchasing a ticket from Penryn to Perran, the young man boarded the 5.45am train from Falmouth to Truro, he was the only occupant of a third class carriage and soon dozed off, not waking until the train had reached the Carnon Viaduct beyond his designated stop at Perran. Realising his mistake, he panicked and flung open the door of the carriage in which he was riding before leaping out onto the track. Landing badly he fell beneath the wheels of the carriage and suffered appalling injuries. No one on the train was aware of the accident and railway labourer James Hender found the horribly mangled printer. His body was lying outside the metals separated from his severed legs that were lying across the track. The victim was conscious and pleaded 'Will you help me?' His rescuer sent for a horse and cart to be used as a makeshift ambulance but within an hour Rillstone passed away before medical assistance could be rendered. The body was conveyed to the Higher Town Inn, near Truro where Coroner Mr Carlyon conducted an inquest the following day. After hearing from one of his employers that the dead man was 'not of strong mind, and was rather eccentric and excitable' the jury concluded that 'the deceased died from injuries he received by jumping from a railway carriage whilst it was in motion on the Cornwall Railway'.

A similar accident occurred on Saturday 18 September 1869. Three young boys from Stoke Damerel had been collecting blackberries and were walking back home across Weston Mill Viaduct, more popularly known as Camel's Head, bridging the creek leading from Hamoaze to Weston Mills. The driver of the 1.55pm train spotted the trespassers on the viaduct between Devonport and Saltash and gave a blast on the whistle as a warning. Half way across the viaduct, the two older boys Maddox and Jarvis, both aged ten, sensibly found refuge in a place of safety at the side of the track but the younger lad, Cruze, aged seven, was frightened and started running alongside the line in front of the engine. Applying the brake but unable to stop in time, the driver James Clatworthy looked on helplessly as the engine passed the boy before his

Children playing near a typical viaduct designed by Brunel at Tregagle

legs were struck by the step of the first carriage. He was knocked over onto the track and the wheels of the carriage passed over the youngster's legs, leaving deep lacerations across the thighs and severing both legs below the knee. In what proved to be a hopeless case, the guard Mr Scantlebury administered first aid. A door was then obtained from a nearby farm and utilised as a stretcher to bear the injured boy as quickly as possible to the Royal Albert Hospital, Devonport. Remaining conscious to the last, Cruze bravely talked about the accident and the nature of his injuries for which the medical staff could do nothing. Two hours after his admission young Cruze died. He was comforted at the end by his father, a boatswain on HMS *Lion*. The Borough Coroner, Mr Bone, held an inquest at the hospital and a verdict of 'Accidental death' was recorded. The jury absolved the railway company of all blame and praised the railwaymen at the scene for their conduct before and after the tragedy.

Four years later, another serious incident took place at Camel's Head Viaduct on 15 April 1873. At 5am a goods train was travelling through the Devonport Tunnel bound for Falmouth, when an axle broke. The train reached the viaduct ripping up the sleepers and rails before the engine and three of the trucks parted company with the remaining fourteen, nine of which ran off the viaduct into the mud below. One end of the viaduct was smashed to pieces and telegraph poles had been badly damaged rendering it impossible to warn a following mail train about the danger. On approaching the viaduct, the startled driver of the mail train saw what had occurred and braked but could not avoid a collision. Fortunately, the only casualty was the second guard of the goods train who suffered several broken ribs.

On Friday 23 June 1871, the death of a well-known and highly respected customs official, which occurred on the line between Penzance and Truro, was reported in melodramatic fashion by a correspondent of the *Western Daily Mercury:*

One of those thrills of horror which excite and unnerve a community, as some sudden and tragic tale passes like wildfire from one to the other member of it, swept through Penzance between two and three o'clock on Friday afternoon, as the news that Mr Barrett, our Collector of Customs, had committed suicide. The news was too true. As the up-train passed, about half-past 12 o'clock, over the Chacewater Viaduct, our fellow town man opened the door of a second-class compartment, of which he was the sole occupant, almost at a single bound was over the parapet, and in five seconds had fallen a hundred feet, and was a mangled corpse.

In actual fact, the article was misleading for Joseph Barrett, a childless widower aged 53, ended his life with a seventy foot leap off Blackwater Viaduct on the Truro side of Chacewater Station. Railway staff rushed to his aid and heard the dying man groan in agony before his suffering quickly ended. As the body fell it had struck one of the timber supports of the viaduct before plunging to the ground, which was covered with piles of rocks and rubble from a disused quarry. Landing spread-eagled on his back, the injuries suffered included deep cuts to the back of the head and lacerations to the face, a broken left leg and a smashed right arm, with bones visibly protruding through the clothing.

The dead man had been on sick leave with a long-term illness and had journeyed a number of times to stay with the family of his brother at Truro. On this occasion he was to be accompanied by a woman who had been acting as his nurse, his cousin Miss Harris, until he dissuaded her from travelling at the last moment. Boarding the 11am from Penzance to Truro, all went well until the train reached Chacewater Station: 'Here, whether the prey of some causeless alarm, or urged by an unhinged mind to end his existence, will be a matter of conjecture; but, while the train moved off slowly, he left it on the giddy viaduct, and with a leap, was in mid-air, and almost instantly afterwards dead'.

The inquest was held at Dingle's Falmouth Arms before Coroner Mr Carlyon. The deceased's superior Alexander Phillips, examining officer of the port of Penzance, identified the body and told the jury: 'I have known him for upwards of fifteen years. I have observed that he became very

Penzance viaduct following the storm damage of 1852

low spirited, suffered from mental depression, and was in a very despondent state. He resumed his duties four weeks this day, after six months' leave of office from congestion of the lungs. He would come into my office and say, "I am quite unable to attend to my duties". At the time he left for Truro he was in great mental agony, and he said he would never be fit for duty again. I got a carriage for him, and put in his things and said I wished I could go with him. Deceased said, "Miss Harris, my cousin is going; that will be all right". I went to the station and got the two tickets, and put the deceased and the lady into a carriage, and stayed with him. After some time deceased said, "I am feeling much better; there is no occasion for Miss Harris to go. Come and see me next week. I am feeling better. See if the stationmaster will take back the ticket"'.

Having been convinced that Joseph Barrett had 'a sick mind in a sick body' the inquest jury had no hesitation in reaching a verdict that the 'Deceased committed suicide whilst in a state of temporary insanity'.

The viaduct at Blackwater was one of nine that were designed by Brunel on the line from Truro stretching twenty-six miles to Penzance where a long low pier-like structure positioned near the station on the exposed shore of Mounts Bay was frequently pounded and damaged by heavy seas. Late on Boxing Day 1852, a terrific storm broke and the following day, gigantic waves washed away a sixty-yard section of timberwork from the end of the 350-yard structure. The line continued after repairs were carried out although services were curtailed in the worst months of the winter season. However, on New Year's Eve 1868, a violent gale at high tide swept away more than half of the structure rendering it derelict. A temporary diversion of the track was installed until a new viaduct was constructed and opened in October 1871.

The Penzance Viaduct was the first of Brunel's timber designs to disappear and the rest were gradually phased out in favour of granite structures to accommodate the changeover from single to a double track operation. During the course of these conversions there were many fatalities including the death of GWR engineer Henry Cole. On Tuesday 1 October 1878, he was supervising the replacement of one of the most impressive wooden structures, Moorswater Viaduct, near Liskeard, when a steam-powered crane unloading a heavy load toppled over. Four tons of stone cascaded down on the engineer crushing him to death. The driver of the travelling crane, Thomas Richards, was badly scalded by boiling water pouring from the overturned steam-driven equipment and was treated for severe burns at East Cornwall Hospital. A hastily convened inquest held later that day heard that the crane weighed fourteen tons and was calculated to lift a five-ton load. The jury viewed the body of the designer of the new viaduct, who was twenty-six years old and left a widow and two children, before recording a verdict of 'Accidental death'.

Although Brunel's imaginative timber viaducts had a frail appearance and often alarmed passengers by noticeably swaying and groaning under the weight of railway vehicles, his designs were never the direct cause of an accident and their strength was proved by a crash which occurred early in the morning on Sunday 11 October 1891. A goods train, due to stop at St Germans to allow a luggage train to pass, ran right through the station 'owing to the slippery state of the line' and was finally brought to a halt a mile beyond on Nottar Viaduct. Frantic efforts to reverse the train back up the steep incline to St Germans failed due to the heavy load and the driver of the stationary goods vehicle was powerless to avoid the oncoming 'down' train from Plymouth resulting in a sickening collision

St Germans Viaduct

33

which wrecked both engines and derailed a number of wagons. Fortunately, no-one was injured and the viaduct remained undamaged which drew this comment from the *West Briton & Cornwall Advertiser*: 'it is somewhat extraordinary that this viaduct, which has been condemned in connection with others on the line, should have withstood the great strain of a collision and that no serious accident followed'.

A far more serious incident occurred at Treviddo Viaduct on Monday 15 November 1897 and was given extensive coverage by the *Western Morning News*:

> *The accident took place at Treviddo, almost midway between Liskeard and Menheniot Stations, where a new five-arch viaduct of granite is being built to take the place of the present one of wood and stone of the type familiar to all travellers on the Cornwall line. The fourth arch from the eastern end is now being turned and wooden ribs were yesterday afternoon in the process of being fixed, on which the brickwork of the arch would rest. There are six ribs in the arch, and the first had been safely positioned and the men were fixing the second, when the accident occurred. About ten minutes past four o'clock the rib had been hoisted into position on the top of the arch by a derrick, and the two men who have now met their death – William Cotton and Richard Toms, both active young fellows – had clambered up to the top of the rib to release the block and chain used in hauling it into place. They accomplished the task, and the rib then remained steadied by a guy rope – a 4-inch mantilla cable. By some means, whether as a result of a sudden squall of wind or some other unlooked for strain, the rope broke. The rib at once turned over towards the present viaduct, and the two men were pre-cipitated into space without a moment's warning and without a chance of saving themselves. They fell a distance of between 75 feet and 80 feet, the rib falling with them, though neither was touched by the mass of woodwork. Cotton, who is only 19 years of age, was killed instantly; but Toms, a man of 32, was alive and conscious when the other workmen hurried to his side. He had fallen upon some of the huge granite blocks used in the construction of the viaduct, and how his life was preserved is a mystery.*

News of the accident was relayed to Menheniot Station and medical aid was summoned by telegraph from Liskeard. A contractor Relf & Sons was carrying out the work for the GWR. They promptly dispatched their company physicians Dr Hammond and Dr Wilson along with two railway porters qualified in first aid. At the scene, young Cotton was beyond help having been pitched on his head and killed instantly. The other casualty Toms was lying at the foot of the viaduct screaming in agony. In addition to appalling internal injuries his left thigh was smashed. The 5pm train from Plymouth was flagged down and the injured man was placed on a stretcher and conveyed to Liskeard. Having survived for an agonising two and a half hours the unfortunate man expired as he was being carried into the Cottage Hospital at 6.40pm.

First impressions that the rib weighing over three tons had collapsed due to a broken guy rope proved to be incorrect. At an inquest conducted at the Stag Hotel, Liskeard, by the Deputy Coroner of Cornwall, Mr De Castro Grubb, it was revealed that when the tragedy occurred foreman Thomas Willcocks was in his office and his deputy Richard Cann was supervising the precarious operation involving four other workmen; railway carpenter Frederick Stephens and general labourers Richard Snell, Thomas Richards and Thomas Harris who were in charge of the guy ropes. The latter workman had charge of the crucial rope hanging below the viaduct, which was secured by being wrapped around a tree and held taut. Instructions to pay out the rope and allow the rib to be hoisted into position by Cotton and Toms were relayed from above by Cann to the carpenter Stephens at ground level who then passed on the information to the waiting Harris. It was evident that for some reason this rope had been released without authority resulting in the deaths of Cotton and Toms.

Supervisor Richard Cann and carpenter Stephens gave damning evidence against Harris who they insisted had been given no fresh instructions for at least five minutes before the accident. After the rope had been hauled into position the men holding the various ropes were told that everything was all right. Cotton and Toms then climbed up the rib to loosen the derrick chain leaving the rib resting correctly on the granite piers, while the ropes on the old viaduct held by Snell and Richards and the one on the tree, held by Harris on the other side were held taut. The operation appeared to have been concluded successfully and the victims required only a few minutes to complete the removal of the derrick chain before descending to safety from the top of the wooden rib when the rib toppled over from the direction of the tree hurling the men to their deaths.

Although cautioned by the Coroner, Thomas Harris answered the criticism by volunteering to give evidence in which he explained that the rope he held was wound once round the tree and as his view of the viaduct was obstructed he took his orders from Stephens standing out in the open nearby. After the derrick chain had been removed Stephens told him to slacken the rope a bit, followed by a second instruction to pay out more rope. He also heard Cann call out, 'Is it all right' to which he replied,

'Yes'. He had the rope held fast in his hand when the rib toppled over. He was shocked and could not understand why it had occurred as he was certain that he had not slackened the rope further.

Foreman Thomas Willcocks confirmed that Harris had given satisfaction whilst working on the project over a period of twelve months and although he had not personally witnessed the accident offered a plausible explanation as to what may have happened. His theory was that Harris overheard a signal from a workman on a travelling crane who was lowering bricks at the same time. The operator was also being given instructions to 'higher' or 'lower' the crane which could have confused Harris.

After deliberating for half an hour the jury concurred and absolved Thomas Harris of blame by returning a verdict of 'Accidental death'. In his summary, the Coroner recalled that it had been his painful duty earlier that year to hold a similar inquiry into an even more horrific tragedy that had shocked the locality. On that occasion several workmen had been killed during the reconstruction of Coldrennick Viaduct, and now, 'Hardly had the thoughts of Coldrennick been forgotten than they had this serious affair at Treviddo, near Coldrennick'.

The incident referred to by the Coroner was a full-scale disaster that occurred on one the highest viaducts in Cornwall at Coldrennick, near Menheniot Station on Tuesday 9 February 1897. Work to widen and strengthen the viaduct had been progressing satisfactorily for two years when catastrophe struck mid-morning. An ill-fated crew of seventeen gangers and labourers were suspended in a cradle beneath one of the central arches to haul a seven hundredweight girder into place when, without warning, the platform fell away and twelve workers were hurled 140 feet to their deaths. The remaining five men miraculously escaped by clinging to the girder or surrounding timberwork and looked down in

Coldrennick Viaduct where twelve workmen were killed in 1897

horror from their lofty perch to see the bodies of their colleagues scattered on the grassy slope below. Those killed were James Harris from Doublebois; Ernest Westaway from Lostwithiel; George Hares from St Germans; Charles Haley and brothers James and William Rundle from Menheniot; James Rowe, Frederick Honey, William Knight, Samuel Bray, Thomas Stephens, William Ede from Liskeard. The fortunate survivors were Samuel Pearse from St Austell, Joseph Penrose from St Germans and William Hill, Samuel Stephens and James Penney from Liskeard.

An improvised mortuary was set up in the goods shed at Menheniot Station where the effect on the grief-stricken community was observed by a correspondent of the *Western Morning News* as they viewed the broken bodies: 'There they were laid out with the most decorous care, side by side. Their hands were folded across their breasts and their faces covered with sacking. Relatives, comrades, and friends soon began to arrive from all quarters, and as one after another of the dead men was identified – some only after great hesitation – the scene was one of the most painful description. Wives sobbed bitterly; father and brothers quivered with the sudden grief which had overwhelmed them.'

The inquest jury inspected the worksite on the viaduct and were shown broken pieces of wood from the platform that appeared to be rotten. In addition the staging supporting the men had not been secured by chains to the main viaduct structure, as was the general rule. Upon retiring to the Sportsmen's Arms, at Menheniot, evidence was heard from ganger Samuel Pearse who had chosen the timber for the platform in the belief that it was of suitable quality and foreman Henry Blewitt who admitted that he had not fixed chains on this occasion and did not feel the procedure was always necessary.

After a deliberation lasting over two hours, the jury returned the following verdict: 'That the cause of the deaths was that while deceased were working on a platform under Coldrennick Viaduct the platform gave way and precipitated them into the valley beneath; and jurors further say that negligence was shown by Foreman Blewitt for not using chains to strengthen the platform, as also by Ganger Pearse for the selection of defective timber in the construction of the said platform; and so jurors do further say the said Blewitt and Pearse did feloniously cause the deaths of the above mentioned twelve persons by neglecting to take proper precautions'.

A magistrates hearing differed in their opinion and found there was no charge for Blewitt and Pearse to answer. At the inquest, the solicitor representing the directors of the GWR had been rebuffed when he had the temerity to ask the jury to add a rider to their verdict that the company be excused from all blame as 'they had made every provision for the safety of the men'. When the Cornwall Assizes opened at Bodmin on Wednesday 16 June, Judge Justice Day made a statement making it absolutely clear that he thought the blame lay squarely with officers of the railway company and was appalled to see two labourers 'earning £1 to 30shillings per week' before the court on a serious charge of manslaughter. In his opinion the lives of twelve men had been sacrificed through gross negligence because the platform was unsafe. The railway company, though responsible civilly, were not responsible criminally. At the same time, their employees might be responsible criminally, though not civilly. The Judge supposed that the GWR Company employed competent men, adequately paid, to supervise work of such importance to the public and their workmen. It appeared to him that these gentlemen thought it was sufficient for them to receive their salaries and leave the work to others. It also seemed that the work had been carried out without proper supervision, which was the cause of the tragedy. He wondered why the accused men should face being sent to penal servitude for life, because those employed to do the work neglected to do so. In summary, his Lordship questioned whether workers of inferior station could be expected to have knowledge of the regulations governing their work. A coroner's jury had acted properly because no other men were brought before them. The magistrates, however, had declined to commit the accused for trial.

Faced with this damning condemnation of their case, the prosecution offered no evidence against Henry Blewitt and Samuel Pearce. Discharging the accused without a stain on their character, there was enthusiastic applause from the public gallery when Judge Day commented caustically that 'It is lamentable that such a disaster caused by gross negligence should remain unpunished'.

The 'Cornwall Disaster' left twenty-five children orphaned and as their fathers were employed as casual labourers, their dependents were not entitled to any compensation. The GWR dealt sympathetically with the immediate financial needs of the families and arranged the funerals, leaving the long term future of the bereaved reliant on a fund launched by the Mayor of Liskeard – prompted by a compassionate letter from Lord St Germans: 'I need hardly say how much Lady St Germans and I have been shocked and grieved by the terrible accident, and how deeply we sympathise with the widows and orphans of the poor men killed. If you should think to start a relief fund at Liskeard I shall be glad to subscribe to it'.

A DIPLOMATIC INCIDENT
Inebriated Youth: 'Hang it, Mister, the paper says a 'Friend'
of yours has been done for murder'
Quaker: 'Thou be assured young sir, yon sinner is no friend of mine'

3

The Killer Kwaker of Slough

The locomotive *North Star* travelled the twenty-five miles from Paddington to Maidenhead carrying a party of VIP's along the first completed section of Brunel's line on Thursday 31 May 1838. A correspondent of *The Sun* was impressed by the journey: 'This railway may well claim for itself the title "great," for it throws completely into the shade all those lines already open to the public'.

A year earlier, a great era in British history had begun when Queen Victoria ascended to the throne. With the arrival of the railroad, famous personalities were able to use the new mode of transport to visit the sovereign at Windsor Castle, which was prominently visible from the GWR line. Amongst those early travellers was the Prime Minister, Sir Robert Peel; one of his predecessors the Duke of Wellington; and notably, Prince Albert of Saxe-Coburg-Gotha, who successfully wooed his cousin resulting in a royal marriage that took place in February1840. The Prince Consort readily embraced train travel, but many advisors considered it

Windsor Castle

was too unsafe for the monarch. Her Majesty was finally coaxed into trying it by her husband on Monday 13 June 1842. The GWR had already built a royal coach in anticipation of the royal patronage and the first train journey of a reigning British monarch was turned into a prestigious event. At noon the royal party left Slough for Paddington with GWR locomotive engineer Daniel Gooch at the controls of the engine accompanied on the footplate by the line's creator Isambard Kingdom Brunel. The scene at Paddington Station was described in the *Windsor and Eton Express:* 'Precisely at 25 minutes past 12 o'clock the Royal Special train entered the terminus having performed the distance in 25 minutes, and on Her Majesty alighting she was given the most deafening demonstrations of loyalty and affection we ever experienced'.

When the Electric Magnetic Telegraph system devised by Wheatstone and Cooke was installed on the line between Slough and Paddington in 1844, it was utilised in August of that year to send a message to the Ministers of the Crown announcing the birth of Queen Victoria and Prince Albert's second son Prince Alfred (known later as the Duke of Edinburgh). The telegraph also proved a useful tool in curtailing criminal activity on trains. Two days before the line from Paddington to Maidenhead opened to the general public on 4 June 1838, the authorities of top public school Eton College, who did not welcome the coming of the railroad, tried to delay matters by applying for an injunction to prevent trains *stopping* in the vicinity of their school at Slough, but the case was dismissed with costs as the GWR legal team argued successfully that the service stopping there did not violate a condition that a station was not then to be provided at Slough. The introduction of the railway was to bring about an end to an ancient school ritual known as the Eton Montem, which was held every three years to raise funds for the senior boy on a foundation scholarship, enabling him to continue his studies at King's College, Cambridge. Members of the Royal Family regularly attended the ceremony when a marching band headed a procession to the ancient religious monument Montem Mound at Salt Hill. Here pupils known as salt-bearers collected money for the cause from visitors. Thousands of extra people flocked to the event by train in 1838 and 1841. As the event now attracted unruly crowds from the lower classes, the Eton Montem was discontinued after 1844, despite the fact that this was also the first occasion that the telegraph was used to fight crime assisting the police to keep a lookout for pickpockets. The telegraph book at Paddington recorded the exchange of police intelligence during the day's successful apprehension of thieves:

Paddington 10.20am. Mail train just started. It contains three thieves, named Sparrow, Burrell and Spurgeon, in the first compartment of the fourth first-class carriage.
Slough 10.50am. Mail train arrived. The officers have cautioned the three thieves.
Paddington 10.50am. Special train just left. It contained two thieves; one named Oliver Martin, who is dressed in black, crape on his hat; the other named Fiddler Dick, in black trousers and light blouse. Both in the third compartment of the first second-class carriage.
Slough 11.16am. Special train arrived. Officers have taken the two thieves into custody, a lady having lost her bag, containing a purse with two sovereigns and some silver in it; one of the sovereigns was sworn to by the lady as having been her property. It was found in Fiddler Dick's watch fob.
Slough 11.51am. Several of the suspected persons who came by the various down trains are lurking about Slough, uttering bitter invectives against the telegraph. Not one of those cautioned has ventured to proceed to the Montem.

The arrest of 'Fiddler Dick' paled into insignificance when the telegraph line was instrumental in bringing a Quaker, John Tawell, to justice for murder. The contribution of the new technology was acknowledged by the *Times*: 'It may be observed, that had it not been for the efficient aid of the electric telegraph, both at Slough and Paddington, the greatest difficulty as well as delay would have occurred in the apprehension of the party now in custody'.

A murder hunt was initiated by these signals sent on New Year's Day 1845. There was no code for the letter 'Q', hence the letter 'K' was substituted and the word 'Quaker' modified to 'Kwaker':

The Wheatstone and Cooke telegraph in operation

Message from Slough:
A murder has just been committed at Salt Hill, and the suspected murderer was seen to take a first-class ticket for London by the train which left Slough at 7.42 p.m. He is in the garb of a Kwaker, with a brown great coat on, which reaches nearly down to his feet; he is in the last compartment of the second first-class carriage.
Reply from Paddington:
The up-train has arrived; and a person answering, in every respect, the description given by telegraph came out of the compartment mentioned. I pointed the man out to Sergeant Williams. The man got into a New Road omnibus, and Sergeant Williams into the same.

Duty Sergeant William Williams of the GWR police sat at the back of the bus and was surprised to be handed a fare by the suspect, who mistook him for the conductor, when he alighted near the Bank of England in Princes Street. Following at a discreet distance the sergeant observed the 'Kwaker' enter the Jerusalem Coffee House, which was a haunt for Australian merchants, then make his way to a lodging house in Scott's Yard which provided accommodation exclusively for members of the Society of Friends. Satisfying himself that the man he was following was settled in for the night, Sergeant Williams returned to Paddington to receive further instructions after ascertaining exactly what had occurred at Salt Hill. It transpired that at about 6.30pm, a woman's screams had been heard coming from one of the four terraced houses in Bath Place. Taking a candle and rushing out of her house to investigate the noise, Mary Anne Ashley heard the front door of the house next door slam shut. Looking round she saw a man she recognised walking up the path. When he opened he gate she asked 'What is wrong with my neighbour; I am afraid she is ill'. The man made no reply and was visibly trembling as he hurried past her. Entering the house, Mrs Ashley, saw her friend Sarah Hart foaming at the mouth and writhing on the floor in agony. A doctor was called but nothing could be done for the victim of cyanide poisoning apparently administered in a glass of porter she had consumed.

The Reverend Champnes, hearing that a man dressed like a Quaker had been seen leaving the scene of a suspicious death, guessed correctly that the suspect must have gone to catch the train to London. He hurried to Slough and seeing a man dressed in a broad brimmed hat, white cravat and long coat, the vicar alerted the railway superintendent of his suspicions. When the Quaker boarded a first class carriage to London, a full description was telegraphed to Paddington and passed to Sergeant Williams.

The following morning, Sergeant Williams, accompanied by Inspector Wiggins of the Metropolitan Police, returned to the lodging house. The suspect had left his room but at lunchtime he was located and arrested at the Jerusalem Coffee House. The man taken into custody was John Tawell, aged sixty-one, who denied having visited Slough or knowing anyone there, but this was soon proved to be untrue. Sarah Hart, a forty-year old mother of two children, a boy and a girl aged five and four respectively, had frequently been visited by Tawell. She told her friends and neighbours that she had worked as a servant for a Quaker couple and married their son against the wishes of his family. The husband was

Paddington Station where Tawell was spotted by Sergeant Williams

working abroad and arranged for the old gentleman Tawell to provide his family with money. This was also untrue, for Sarah Hart was unmarried and the father of her two children was none other than her elderly visitor and former employer John Tawell. The Quaker's life had been a litany of misdemeanours strangely at odds with his pious beliefs.

Born near Norwich in Norfolk, John Tawell had been introduced to the Society of Friends at the age of fourteen whilst working in a shop owned by a Quaker widow. Six years later he was working at a draper's shop in the Whitechapel area of London, owned by another Quaker, where he began a relationship with a serving girl called Mary who was soon expecting his child. The Quaker faith strongly disapproved of this lewd behaviour by two members of their community and the shamed lovers entered into belated wedlock. The couple had two sons before Tawell committed a sin against the Quaker community, which also violated the law of the land for which the penalty was death.

Whilst working as a travelling salesman for a chemist, Tawell was committed for trial on charges connected with the forgery of banknotes. He had been arrested after trying to pass himself off as a partner of Smith's Bank of Uxbridge. Boldly visiting the bank's engraver he ordered a new plate to be made and 'specimens' of £5 notes bearing the name of Smith's Bank to be printed. When the customer was satisfied with the proofs he placed an order for a quantity of notes. By now the engraver's suspicions were aroused and when Tawell returned to pay the bill and collect the banknotes, the police were laying in wait and apprehended the fraudster as he left the shop. The owners of the bank were Quakers and this crime committed by one of their number left them in a quandary. The Society of Friends was opposed to the death penalty that Tawell now faced, as forgery was then a capital offence. The Smith family were relieved of the responsibility for such harsh justice and did not press charges when a forged banknote belonging to the Bank of England was found on Tawell's person. The accused was charged with 'feloniously falsely forging and counterfeiting a Bank-note for payment of 10 shillings [50p], with intent to defraud the Governor and Company of the Bank of England'.

When Tawell appeared at the Old Bailey on 4 February 1814, an admission to a lesser offence of 'possession' was accepted and the prisoner was considered extremely fortunate to avoid execution for forgery and fraud. As a consequence a comparatively 'lenient' sentence of fourteen years transportation was imposed. For the first few years of his sentence, the prisoner was assigned to labouring on coal ships working around the coast of Australia. His knowledge of medicines, learned while working for the chemist in London, won him a position in a convict hospital, fol-

lowed by a spell at the Sydney Academy as a clerk. The principal, Isaac
Wood, was impressed by the convict's faith and intelligence and peti-
tioned for Tawell's parole, which was granted half way through the sentence in 1820. With his unexpected freedom, Tawell then displayed aston-
ishing entrepreneurial flair by establishing a successful business as a
chemist and druggist in Sydney. From this base he quickly amassed a
personal fortune of over £20,000 from land, property and the shipping
trade. Although, aligning himself closely with the local Quaker community in Sydney, his conscience was apparently not troubled by taking a
mistress in the colony until his wife and children sailed out to join him in
1823. The couple added a daughter to their family and decided to return
to England in November 1831. John Tawell had earned wealth and
respectability and was given a warm send-off by his business associates
which was reported by the *Sydney Gazette*:

*On the evening of Saturday last, about 20 respectable colonists gave a
farewell dinner, at Hart's tavern, to Mr. Tawell, an old and esteemed resi-
dent in Sydney, who is about to return to England by the first vessel. Mr.
Samuel Terry presided on the occasion, and was well supported by Mr.
Simpson Lord as vice-president. After the cloth was removed, and the usual
loyal toasts were drunk, the president after some appropriate remarks, pro-
posed the health of Mr. Tawell, who returned thanks for the honour con-
ferred upon him by so many respectable gentlemen, assuring the company
that whether he should return to the colony, or remain in England, the rec-
ollection of their kindness would ever be to him one of the greatest pleasures
of his life. The health of Mrs. Tawell and family was also drunk, and
acknowledgements in suitable terms by Mr. Tawell. Several songs were
sung in the course of the evening, and the company broke up about 11
o'clock, after enjoying one of the most convivial parties ever witnessed in
the colony. The object of the entertainment, that of paying a well-deserved
tribute of respect to an old colonist, now about to bid perhaps a final adieu
to our shores, was not more creditable to the guest than to those by whom
so high a compliment was paid to him. We ought to add, that Mr. Hart, by
providing a very excellent dinner, contributed his share to the enjoyment of
the evening.*

There were tragic consequences of the family's return to England. The
appalling social conditions in Victorian London affected the health of the
Tawell's youngest son William who died in 1833. The following year the
bereaved parents returned to Australia and in 1837 the first Friends
Meeting House opened in Sydney with a plaque bearing the donor's

name 'John Tawell – to the Society of Friends'. The Tawell's final journey home in July 1838 coincided with the death of their married son John, who had remained in England to train as a doctor. This blow was too much to bear for the grief stricken Mary Tawell who became gravely ill and her husband employed a young nurse Sarah Lawrence to care for his wife at their home in Berkhampstead, Hertfordshire. As Mary's life ebbed away, Tawell turned for comfort to Sarah and soon after his wife's death the servant girl was expecting his child and moved away to give birth to a son called Frederick. The name of the father was kept secret but Tawell continued seeing Sarah and when she became pregnant again, it was an inconvenience to the religious hypocrite, who by this time planned to marry a highly respectable widow, Sarah Cutworth, a Quaker who ran a school for young ladies. After giving birth to a daughter she named after herself, Sarah changed her name to Hart and agreed to shield her master from embarrassment by moving to Slough. For her trouble she received an allowance from the children's father of £1.00 a week.

Tawell's criminal past meant that he had never been fully accepted back into the fold by the London Society of Friends despite his numerous acts of generosity to worthy causes. Despite the warnings of her friends and family in the Quaker community, the widow Cutworth gave up her school and married Tawell at a registry office in February 1841. The marriage was not sanctioned by the Quaker movement, therefore both partners of the union were designated 'outward court worshippers'. Living with the newly-weds was a daughter from each of their previous marriages and soon the family had an addition when the couple produced a son. Increasingly, Tawell was worried that his illicit relationship with a former servant might come to light. He was overdrawn at the bank while experiencing difficulties with his business interests in Australia and decided to use his knowledge of poisons to eliminate one of his financial burdens – Sarah Hart.

The first attempt to kill his former lover ended in failure. During a visit to deliver maintenance in September 1844, Sarah vomited after drinking a glass of stout, which she believed she had drunk too quickly, not knowing that it contained a drug administered by her malevolent benefactor. Next time, the murderer made sure his evil intention was successfully carried out. On 1 January 1845, Tawell entered a chemist's shop in Bishopsgate Street and purchased a preparation normally prescribed to treat varicose veins that contained deadly prussic acid (cyanide). Travelling across London to Paddington, he caught the 4pm train to Slough and went to see his secret family at their home in Salt Hill. Sarah was pleased to see him, as her quarterly allowance was overdue. She went out to the nearby Windmill Hotel, purchased a bottle of Guinness and borrowed a corkscrew opener, which she promised, 'You may depend on my returning in the morning'. The stout was poured into two glasses and Tawell managed to distract Sarah long enough to lace the drink with a lethal dose of poison that took immediate effect. The killer paused to take back his maintenance money then fled from the scene. After boarding the 7.42 to Paddington his carefully planned escape was foiled by the smart use of the telegraph system. Unaware of the fact that he had been shadowed, Tawell protested his innocence when arrested at the Jerusalem Coffee House assuring the officers 'I wasn't at Slough yesterday'. Sergeant Williams replied, 'Yes you were sir, you got out of the train and got into an omnibus and gave me the change'. Seemingly unphased by this revelation, Tawell confidently retorted, 'You must be mistaken in the identity; my station in society will be sufficient to rebut any suspicion against me'.

Once in the custody of the Eton police, Tawell admitted knowing the victim and suggested that she had committed suicide in a statement to Superintendent Perkins:

That wretched and unfortunate woman once lived in my service for nearly two years and a half. I was pestered with letters from her when I was in London and I determined to give her no more money. She was a bad woman – a very bad woman. She sent me a letter threatening to do something. She said she would make away with herself if I did not give her any money. I went down to her house and told her I would not give her any more money. She then asked me to give her a drop of porter. She had a glass, and I had a glass. She held in her hand over the glass of porter a very small phial, not bigger than her finger and said, 'I will, I will!' She poured something out of the phial into the stout and drank part of it. She then lay down on the rug and I walked out. I should not have gone out if I thought she had been in earnest. I certainly should not have left her.

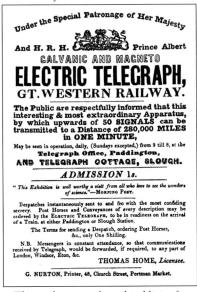

The trial attracted good publicity for the electric telegraph

The Trial opened at the Buckinghamshire Assizes held at Aylesbury County Court on 12 March 1845 presided over by Judge Baron Parke. The prosecution produced a witness who knew the full story of the secretive affair between master and servant. Charlotte Howard, a carpenter's wife from Paddington, was a friend of Sarah's and had visited the couple's first love nest in Bridge Street, Southwark: 'I knew Sarah Hart. About six years ago she went to nurse the first Mrs Tawell. Mrs Tawell died about nine or ten weeks after she went to nurse her, and deceased remained in the service of the prisoner.

'About five years ago she told me she was in the family way. I remember on one occasion taking tea there with the prisoner. Sarah brought in the tea and took the things away again. She then came in and sat down by my side. I said I know Sarah what you are going to speak about. She got up and showed a disposition to vindicate her master. In June 1840, he said he was about to get married to Mrs Cutworth and if these things were rumoured about it would make a very great difference. He laughed and begged Sarah not to excite herself so much; he said he was about to be admitted as a Friend, and should not like her latest pregnancy to be talked about. She said she would be dead to the world from that time; that no-one would know what became of her, not even her own mother'.

The jury heard how two visits from Tawell had affected Sarah Hart's health. The victim had supplemented her income by caring for the illegitimate child of servant Charlotte Howard who was staying with Sarah on the first occasion that she had been taken poorly: 'On 26 September 1843 I went to stay with Mrs Hart at Bath Place. I was then in the family way and gave birth there. I remained there four months. During that time I saw Mr Tawell two or three times. I went to the house last September again. My child was there. I got leave of absence from my mistress to go and see my child for a fortnight. I remember Mr Tawell coming down on the 30 September 1844, shortly before 7pm in the evening. I did not see him but heard his voice. He stayed there about 40 minutes.

'I was told by Mrs Hart to go and get a bottle of porter, which I did. I then saw Mrs Hart again; she came out of the room and said "I am very ill, I was obliged to tell my master to go, for I can scarce stand". She looked dreadfully pale and ill, retched a good deal, and complained about being sick in the head. Before that she was in sound health. She went upstairs and partly recovered by taking rest; but in the night she again complained of being sick, and retched much. She retched altogether about a full hand basin. She said she had drunk a glass of porter, and she was sorry she had drunk it all at once, for it had affected her head immediately, and made her feel very giddy. On coming downstairs I observed on the table in the room where Mr Tawell had been: 13 sovereigns, half a bottle of porter and two glasses. I drank some of the remaining porter but it did not make me feel sick'.

First on the scene of the murder was widow Mary Anne Ashley who heard the victim's screams and saw Tawell leave before she entered the house to witness Sarah Hart's death throes: 'I found her lying upon her back on the floor, with her clothes nearly up to her knees, and the stocking on her left leg nearly down and torn. Her cap was off her head, and she appeared to have been struggling. She was alive and making a moaning cry. I bathed her temples with vinegar and water. On the table in the room were a bottle and a tumbler, both containing some beer, and also a jug of water. When I lifted her up she was foaming at the mouth. Another neighbour, Mrs Barrett, came in and used the empty glass to give water to the deceased. I said, "She cannot swallow; don't give her any, it will choke her"'.

Tawell objected to paying £1.00 a week to support his illegitimate family but spared no expense on his legal costs that were estimated to be in excess of £700. He engaged eminent advocate Sir Fitzroy Kelly who had tears in his eyes as he made an emotional plea to the jury on behalf of an 'innocent man'. After first suggesting that the deceased may have been poorly and choked to death when the neighbour poured water down her throat, he also came up with an alternative suspect in his address to the jury – apple pips!

A post mortem examination had revealed pieces of undigested apple in the victim's stomach. As minute traces of cyanide are present in apple pips, the devious lawyer attempted to convince the court that a diet of too much fruit over the festive season had brought about the premature death of Sarah Hart: 'What were the jury called upon to believe? A woman in health had died suddenly, and the prosecutor asked the jury to take away the life of the prisoner on the supposition that she had died from prussic acid and not any one of the many causes of sudden death. What was the quantity of prussic acid required to cause death? It might be un-dissolved apples, bitter almonds or anything else containing prussic acid. I wish to impress upon the jury, that, next to bitter almonds, there is no substance which contains more prussic acid than the pips of apples, the quantity differing according to the nature of the apple'.

This revelation was said to have had a detrimental affect on the sale of apples, but the jury were unimpressed by this explanation. The jurors already had the 'pip' and complained to the Judge about the standard of their accommodation where there were no beds and they had been forced to sleep on the floor. After putting up with this nightly discomfort and hearing evidence for three days they retired to consider their verdict and required only half-an-hour for their deliberations before they returned a verdict of 'Guilty'.

Unlike members of the jury, the condemned man was provided with a bed; in fact he was chained to it throughout his confinement, but nevertheless, observed the proprieties by writing a letter of thanks to the Governor of Aylesbury Prison, Mr Sheriff:

Dear and worthy friend, Mr. Sheriff, It is not less my duty to than great pleasure, as well as from feelings of deep and sincere gratitude, that I can thus offer my poor but unqualified thanks to both thyself and poor Mrs. Sheriff for the continued and marked kind attention which has been shown so uniformly to myself and my dear and valuable family and friends since my unfortunate confinement in this prison, by allowing us all the access which urbanity and philanthropy could suggest, under such circumstances, to the participants in this severe affliction.

And now their deeply distressing probation is nearly concluded, I have to desire that this may be accepted as the most grateful acknowledgement, both on account of myself and them.

I can desire myself that the Divine blessing may largely rest on thyself, and Mrs. Sheriff, and your family; and my own valuable family will lastingly have to re-echo this poor but sincere benediction of thy faithful but afflicted friend. John Tawell.

The Governor and the Prison Chaplain, the Reverend Cox, sat up praying with Tawell on the night before his execution. Having convinced his wife, brother and concerned members of the Society of Friends that he was totally innocent of the charge, the sanctimonious killer kept up the pretence to visitors right up to the day of the execution. At 5am the governor reminded the condemned man that his time was drawing near and broached the subject of a confession, 'Mr Tawell, I think there was some promise made me of a statement you intended leaving'. The prisoner replied, 'If I promised then I will do so' and produced a piece of paper, which he gave to the chaplain with the proviso that the contents should not be made public. He then sat down in the cell and admitted: 'Yes, I am guilty of the crime. I put the prussic acid into the porter, and I also attempted the crime in September last, not by prussic acid, but morphia'.

Hangman William Calcraft was appointed to conduct the public execution at 8am on Friday 28 March. A temporary scaffold was erected by fixing a platform on top of the iron railings of the balcony at the county hall that stood alongside the prison. Pressmen noted that there was a disappointing turnout of only 'two or three thousand persons present' mainly 'agricultural workers' and women of 'questionable character'. The crowd were kept waiting for over twenty minutes after the appointed hour before the bewildered figure of the condemned man was pushed out into view by a turnkey. The prisoner, still attired in the dress of a Quaker, clasped his handcuffed hands together and dropped to one knee continually repeating a brief prayer, 'Sweet Jesus, receive my spirit', before being hauled to his feet by the impatient Calcraft. The undignified proceedings were described by a correspondent of the *Times*:

When the fixing of the rope had been properly completed... the executioner and the turnkey withdrew into the hall, and the bolts sustaining the platform on which the wretched man stood were instantly pulled back, and he fell; but the length of the drop allowed him was so little, that he struggled most violently. His whole frame was convulsed; he writhed horribly, and his limbs rose and fell again repeatedly, while he continued to wring his hands for several minutes, they still being clasped as though he had not left off praying. It was nearly ten minutes after the rope had been fixed before the contortions, which indicated his extreme suffering ceased. ... He died

Strangers on a train: 'the historic crime stimulated rare comment in a railway carriage'

"hard," as the phrase is; and his light body dangled in the breeze, backwards and forwards, and round about, a most pitiable and melancholy spectacle. … And the removal of the body was quite consistent with the rest of the revolting exhibition, for it was not cut down, but the turnkey held up the legs while the executioner, untied the rope, which was certainly a new cut, and probably considered worth saving for some purpose or other.

The sensational nature of the case provided excellent publicity for the Wheatstone and Cooke invention and the telegraph offices at Slough and Paddington became an extremely popular visitor attraction as the public, 'who dearly love anything connected with a murder, flocked to see the new apparatus at work, cheerfully paying their shillings [5p] for the privilege of doing so'. A former Lieutenant-Governor of Canada, Sir Francis Head, also recalled that the historic crime stimulated rare comment in a railway carriage: 'A few months afterwards, we happened to be travelling by rail from Paddington to Slough in a carriage filled with people all strangers to one another. Like English travellers they were all mute. For nearly fifteen miles no one had uttered a single word, until a short-bodied, short-necked, short-nosed, exceedingly respectable-looking man in the corner, fixing his eyes on the apparently fleeting posts and wires of the electric telegraph, significantly nodded to us as he muttered aloud –"Them's the cords that hung John Tawell."'

CRIMINAL BEHAVIOUR
'Let's go to the 'anging and 'ave a laff'

The Great Western Train Robbery
& The Bermondsey Murder

On New Year's Day 1849, an audacious robbery took place on the 6.35pm Plymouth to London mail train. The perpetrators of the crime, Henry Poole and Edward Nightingale, boarded a first-class carriage and during the journey between Exeter and Bristol gained entry to the unguarded mail van and helped themselves to property valued at over £150,000 which was disposed of and never recovered. The crooks then impudently attempted a repeat performance on the return journey. The mail sacks were found to have been tampered with at Bridgewater and following a search of the train, incriminating evidence was discovered. The pair were then arrested on suspicion and detained at Exeter. The case attracted national interest and featured a banner headline in the *Times*: 'Extraordinary Robbery On The Great Western Railway'.

Edward Nightingale was 'wanted' for another undisclosed crime and refused to give his name. He was not identified until the commencement of the Magistrates Hearing at Exeter Guildhall, when Detective-sergeant Edward Langley of Scotland Yard appeared in court and confirmed that the defendant was a 'horse dealer' from Hoxton, London, and well known to the police. Nightingale's father George, who had died about six months earlier, was also a villain. He had been a bookmaker at

Goodwood and according to the press had 'obtained considerable notoriety by his gambling transactions'. Like his son, Nightingale senior was also a mail robber; in 1827 he was acquitted of robbing the Dover to London stagecoach after producing witnesses to say that on the night of the crime he had been in the Three Tuns tavern at Tiverton, near Exeter. However, as he was leaving the Maidstone courthouse, he was arrested for another highway robbery, committed two years earlier in Warwick.

The *Illustrated London News* discovered that, 'Poole belongs to a respectable family from Taunton, but has not been on friendly terms with them since he commenced his present plundering pursuits'. Nine months before the robbery, Poole had seemingly come into a fortune and, according to conflicting reports; either resigned or was discharged from his job as a GWR guard. He took an elegant residence in Exeter with twenty 'superbly furnished' rooms and soon after his arrest instructed 'friends' to sell his valuable effects. The *Exeter Gazette* reported that special catalogues were printed and the lots attracted high bids over two whole sales days. The auctioneer remarked that the 'furniture was fit for the mansion of any nobleman'. Despite his wealthy lifestyle, further funded by lucrative money lending activities, Poole could not resist the lure of easy money and risked his liberty for a treasure trove utilising 'inside knowledge' gained while he was a guard on the mail trains. Planning had taken months and Poole had experimented with various disguises to avoid being recognised by his former railway colleagues as explained in *Trewman's Exeter Flying Post*:

> *Since his retirement from the Great Western, Poole has frequently appeared in the streets of Exeter in singular costume; in many cases most grotesquely attired; and it has been on many occasions observed that he has travelled up and down the line dressed in this style. ... Three or four months since, when dressed as a labouring man, he was found in what is technically called 'the locker' of a railway carriage (the place in which the parcels are deposited), but little or no suspicion was excited on account of the plausible excuses which the man offered for his conduct.*

Donning false moustaches and unfamiliar garb – Nightingale wearing a reversible coat of contrasting colours and Poole, a cloak with a high collar and a green felt broad rimmed hat – the felons put their plan into action at Starcross. After having a drink at the Courtenay Arms, positioned alongside Brunel's recently abandoned Atmospheric Engine House, they bought one-way tickets on the station and boarded the night train, seating themselves in one of the private compartments of the spacious broad gauge first class carriage behind the mail tender. Poole knew from experience, that while the train was travelling between Exeter and Bristol, the guard left the mail van unattended to assist the clerks in the sorting of letters on the adjoining Travelling Post Office. With no stop between Bridgewater and Bristol, there was a window of opportunity allowing the thieves a little over one hour to make their way precariously along the footboards on the outside of the train, using a hook to secure a hold on the top of the carriage, then enter the mail van and plunder the sealed bags containing registered letters and bankers parcels. The heist was a complete success and they apparently disposed of their plunder to the keeping of unknown accomplices at Bristol, then shortly after midnight had a celebratory drink of brandy and water in the Talbot Inn before calmly purchasing tickets for the return journey. Greed was to be their downfall; for they could have escaped unnoticed and got clean away as pandemonium ensued when the rifled bags were discovered by baffled railway staff, with no clues to help the investigation that was immediately instigated.

By coincidence, a passenger on the 'down' train was Superintendent Joseph Gibbons of Plymouth police. At Bridgewater, guards informed him that the mailbags had been robbed. Realising that the thieves must still be on-board the train, he ordered a search of the carriages at Taunton. Poole and Nightingale, seated suspiciously with the blinds drawn in a compartment of the first-class carriage, were quickly rumbled when a dozen packages were found under their seats wrapped in a shawl together with false moustaches, crepe masks, hook, string, candle and sealing wax. When questioned about the booty both men replied, 'We know nothing about it'. They also denied knowing each other and Nightingale attempted to bluff his way out of trouble by insisting, 'I am a respectable man and have fifty men in my employ'. As they were arrested on suspicion, under-guard John Thomas saw through the disguise of his former colleague and called out; 'That's Harry Poole'.

The thieves returned to Exeter, not as rich men, but prisoners. The key to the failure of their plan was highlighted in evidence given by Leonard Barrett, mail guard on the 'down' train. He explained that when Poole had worked for the GWR, the oil lamps of the mail van were fixed on the inside of the doorway. Recently, these had been replaced by roof lamps, which made it impossible for the felons to use the candle and wax found in their possession. It was evident that they had intended to light the candle from the lamp and melt the wax to reseal the bags and prevent all possibility of detection until the bags reached their final destination. Instead, the bags were merely re-tied with string and the theft was readily discovered on the outward journey when the train reached Bristol, not London. Without this hitch their plan would have bought them more time to plunder the 'down' train but Poole and Nightingale did not assess the risk, or merely ignored the possibility, that the railway guards had been alerted to the fact that a robbery had taken place when they reported for duty on the return train at Bristol and were bound to be extra vigilant.

Counsel for the defendants in his closing argument intimated that entry to the mail tender from the first-class carriage in the dark was far too dangerous to contemplate on a train travelling at speeds up to 50mph, 'Why a cat could not have done it.' However, the jury had already heard how intrepid mail guard Leonard Barrett had proved otherwise in a risky re-enactment: 'I have made a trial to ascertain if anyone could pass from the first-class carriage to the Post-office tender. I did so … on the down train between Bristol and Bridgewater. I proceeded from the door of the third compartment of the first-class carriage along the steps, then over the buffers of the carriage and tender, taking hold of the handles of the parcels department, on to the step of the Post-office van, and then walked along the steps and lifted the window with my nail, and then got in. I did this while the train was in motion'.

The trial, attended by leading figures from the Great Western, Bristol & Exeter and South Devon railway companies, commenced on Friday 23 March at the Spring Assizes held at Exeter Castle. The prosecution had insufficient evidence to connect Poole and Nightingale with the 'up' train robbery, from which valuables were missing, estimated in excess of £150,000. However, this appears to be a highly inflated figure as the prisoners faced charges for the theft of only £150 worth of miscellaneous articles from the 'down' train including: twelve letters, six rings, a watchcase and gold ring mountings. Nevertheless, the stealing of any property belonging to HM Postmaster General could result in transportation for life. The jury took only half-an-hour to return a verdict of 'Guilty' against both prisoners. The Judge, Lord Denman, commended the jury on their deliberation before addressing the accused: 'The evidence is so strong and overpowering that to have said you were not guilty would have been inviting others to commit similar crimes. What can one think when a discharged guard, who comes to Exeter with no apparent motive, meets another man with no honest calling, goes to Starcross and starts to Bristol, returns by the next train, comes and conceals himself, and tells a false story? The mere fact of your being present with all that knowledge and so conducting yourself, and the disappearance of the letters, would be strong enough to show that you two were the men, and you Poole, with your evident activity and skill, concealment, disguise and falsehood, bear the strongest evidence of guilt; you must be transported for fifteen years'. During the trial of the foiled train robbers, it became evident that the GWR had been tipped off about the criminals' intentions some months earlier by two respectable Taunton men, Eales White, proprietor of the East Reach Brewery and surgeon James Dyer. Details of a 'remarkable prophecy' were revealed by *Trewman's Exeter Flying Post*: 'We are in a position to assert an extraordinary fact connected with these Jack Sheppard-like achievements … The information was given … by the wife of one of the supposed accomplices in this and many other "railway schemes"'. The *Taunton Courier* confirmed the story:

> *The communication was made most circumstantially to the persons named as to the mode in which the late robbery was to be effected, and the description of the disguise to be used was minutely described, even to the 'moustaches' found in the railway carriage occupied by the prisoners. … the communication was made by the wife of the man said to be implicated in the robbery while in a paroxysm of anger arising from the ill-usage she had experienced. He had, consistently with his accustomed brutality, turned her out of his house, and it was while she was consulting those to whom she had appealed for advice that the various and long-continued enormities of her husband had been disclosed.*

The woman who revealed the secret of the conspiracy was Maria Manning, the vexed wife of Frederick Manning, landlord of the White Hart Inn, Taunton, where the train robbery had been planned. It was no

Haldon House the home of Lord and Lady Palk

coincidence that the publican's closest friend was Henry Poole. Before entering the licensed trade, Manning had been employed as a GWR guard and had first met lady's maid Maria when she regularly accompanied her mistress Lady Palk on the London train from Exeter, where her ladyship resided on the outskirts of the city at Haldon House. Although there was not enough evidence upon which to proceed with a prosecution, Manning was apparently dismissed by the GWR when suspected of being involved in a spate of thefts culminating in the mysterious disappearance of gold valued at £5,000 on 10 January 1848. It appears that both Poole and Manning may have parted company with the GWR following an internal investigation into this affair when the *Times* announced developments at Taunton, 'Several of the company's servants from the station where the suspected persons alighted were brought up and examined, and it is said that circumstances have transpired that will eventually lead to the apprehension of the parties implicated in the robbery'. The bullion box had been loaded at Paddington bound for Taunton, but when a superintendent at Bristol inspected it, the entire contents had been removed by gaining entry to the box 'dextrously cut by means of a circular saw, or similar instrument, and the work was that of some practiced hands'. The carriage adjoining that 'in which the treasure was deposited', was occupied by 'six persons of fashionable appearance', whom the police believed were criminals belonging to the London 'swell mob' of which, it later transpired, Edward Nightingale was a prominent member. This particular crime may been the one for which the villain was sought by the police and the reason why he refused to confirm his name until identified by a detective at Exeter Assizes in 1849.

Fortunate to be released after facing police questioning about their role in the latest train robbery, Frederick and Maria Manning, who had incurred debts and lost the White Hart Inn during their marriage wrangles, settled in Bermondsey. They rented a house at Miniver Place, which, they planned to share with a previous suitor of Maria's called Patrick O'Connor. According to author Robert Huish who published a series of broadsides recording *The Authentic Memoirs of Maria Manning*, in 1849, they had met seven years earlier when Maria (born Marie de Roux, at Geneva in 1821) was working at an inn where she met Patrick when he was in service with an Irish family named Wentworth who were holidaying in Switzerland. Although more than twice her age, Patrick was immediately smitten with the girl and persuaded his employers that she would be suitable for the position of lady's maid. Therefore, Maria returned to the couple's mansion of Ballincraig in County Kilkenny, where her affair with Patrick ended suddenly when Mr Wentworth caught the lovers locked in a passionate embrace and dismissed the aggrieved O'Connor. Further scandal ensued when Mrs Wentworth's suspicions were also aroused and upon 'opening the door of the library in the softest manner', discovered 'her beloved and continent husband sitting on the sofa with her chaste and immaculate servant affectionately seated on his knee'. The outraged Mrs Wentworth flew at the shamed girl and scratched her face before ordering the 'vicious, abominable hussy' from her household. Maria's next position ended with the premature death of Lady Palk in January 1846. With glowing references from her ladyship's widowed husband, Devonshire landowner and Member of Parliament, Sir Lawrence Palk, she moved to London as a lady's maid to Lady Ballantyre, the daughter of the Duke and Duchess of Sutherland, at the majestic Stafford House, near Buckingham Palace. Later that year she renewed her acquaintance with Patrick O'Connor whilst travelling across the Channel to Boulogne to join her new mistress. The forty-eight year old from Tipperary, had come up in the world and was taking a break from his job as a customs officer in the London Docks. This was an ironic profession for someone who regularly abused his position with smuggling activities of his own, whilst also dabbling in fraud by demanding payment to help job seekers find employment in the docks. O'Connor also built up a lucrative money-lending venture among his work colleagues and invested the profits in foreign railway stocks.

Both O'Connor and Manning wanted to marry Maria, but she chose the latter, swayed by news of a £400 inheritance received following the death of his father, a former sergeant in the Somerset militia, who later ran The Bear public house in Taunton. A stylish wedding was arranged and took place at St James Church, Piccadilly in June 1847. When O'Connor learned of the marriage he was devastated and wrote an anguished letter to Stafford House: 'Ah, Maria! You have acted cruelly to me. Why not, like a true professor of what you avowed, write and say what you intended before you acted so, then, at the risk of losing my situation, I would have gone every step that man could, and got married to the only being on the face of the earth who could make me happy'.

Frederick Manning

Frederick Manning was soon to rue winning Maria's hand. His choice of bride did not altogether impress members of his family and the groom belatedly admitted to his brother Edmund, 'I should never have married that woman if I had listened to your advice'. Following the GWR guard's dismissal from his job, the marriage foundered and after informing on the train robbery plotters, Maria took the White Hart's takings and fled to revive her affair with O'Connor in London. Later reconciled with Manning, who, if involved in the GWR robbery had clearly not profited greatly from it, the pair had no visible means of support and they conspired to kill O'Connor and relieve him of his considerable wealth. The two men appeared to be on good terms despite their rivalry for Maria's affection. Frederick even offered to let Patrick move in at Miniver Place to share the rent (and possibly Maria in a ménage a trios). O'Connor reneged on the agreement causing the Mannings to temporarily take in a medical student as a lodger. Maria easily manipulated the two men in her life and she appears to have taken the lead in the murder plot. The foul deed was committed on Thursday 9 August 1849, when O'Connor accepted an invitation to dine at Miniver Place. The couple purchased implements in preparation for the crime; Frederick bought a pistol and a crowbar, while Maria obtained a shovel and took delivery of some quicklime. A hole was dug beneath flagstones in the basement kitchen, in which to bury the body. After leaving work at the docks, O'Connor walked unsuspectingly to his death at Miniver Place. When he arrived for dinner, Maria led him to the kitchen past the hole, which she said had been excavated for work on the drains. As her guest washed his hands and face in the sink, she coldly produced a pistol and shot him in the back of the head. O'Connor still showed

signs of life so Frederick then finished him off with seventeen blows to the head delivered with the crowbar. The victim was then stripped of his clothes before his arms and legs were bent back and trussed to the trunk with rope. The corpse was then dropped face down into the pit, treated with quicklime to eat the body away, before the flagstones were replaced and re-plastered with cement to conceal all trace of wrong-doing. The couple then calmly sat down to dine and heartily ate the goose that Maria had ostensibly cooked for three people.

Maria Manning

Maria Manning had been a frequent visitor to O'Connor's lodgings over a shop in Mile End. The landlady had been instructed by her tenant to allow Maria to enter his rooms at any time. Armed with a key to a cashbox removed from the dead man's pocket, Maria wasted no time to collect the valuables that had made O'Connor such a good marriage prospect. She quickly helped herself to £4,000 in cash, share certificates and foreign railway stocks. Two days later, Frederick impersonated O'Connor to trade some shares and called in at a bank to obtain change for a £100 note. Meanwhile, O'Connor's colleagues reported him missing when he did not turn up for work and the police made enquiries at Miniver Place. The Mannings denied any knowledge of their friend's whereabouts and claimed that their guest must have changed his mind for he had not arrived at the arranged time. However, when the police called again, the murderers panicked and fled their home on Monday 13 August. That same day, a cousin of O'Connor's, William Flynn, visited the moneylender's rooms and discovered that his cashbox had been looted. Hurrying round to Miniver Place he learned that Maria had left in a hansom cab with several large trunks. The following day, second-hand dealer Charles Bainbridge who had paid Frederick Manning £13 for the furniture, emptied the house. The police did not suspect foul play until a thorough search of the house was conducted on Friday 17 August. Two police officers noticed the extra tidiness of the kitchen and the fresh

The gruesome discovery of the murder

cement on the floor. They called in some workmen to lift the flagstones and made the gruesome discovery of O'Connor's decomposed body.

A hue and cry ensued. The hunt was now on for the perpetrators of the crime. A watch was put on ports, as it was believed that Maria would attempt to return to mainland Europe, but she had travelled in a first class train carriage to Edinburgh. She was apprehended in the Scottish capital after arousing suspicion by trying to sell the foreign railway stocks she had stolen from O'Connor. A stockbroker noted the address of her hotel and informed the police of her whereabouts. When she was arrested, her baggage was searched revealing cash totalling £188. Her foreign accent had given her away to the stockbroker who was alerted because she foolishly tried to pass herself off as the daughter of a Glaswegian named Robertson. More than a third of the money in her possession was savings accrued by her husband Frederick who had been left penniless and abandoned to his fate by his scheming spouse. With only the proceeds of the furniture, he journeyed on the train from Waterloo to Southampton and took the midnight ferry to Jersey. Staying at a hotel in St Helier, he tried to pass himself off as a gin salesman, but his favourite tipple proved to be brandy and his heavy drinking and vulgar behaviour attracted unwanted attention. When he saw a man he recognised from his hometown of Taunton, Frederick left St Helier, wisely deciding to keep a low profile by renting rooms in a property in the country called Prospect Cottage. The rent was four shillings (20p) a week, although his money was rapidly diminishing as he continually downed alcohol, doubtless in an effort to wipe out the memory of the brutal death of his love rival and the subsequent betrayal by his duplicitous wife. Alerted to the fugitive's presence on the island, Detective-sergeant Edward Langley, who had previously identified Edward Nightingale for the criminal court and interviewed the Mannings to ascertain what they knew about the GWR robbery, travelled to Jersey accompanied by another officer from Scotland Yard. On Monday 27 August, after two and a half weeks at large, Manning was roused from his sleep and arrested as he lay in bed. His immediate reaction was to enquire, 'Is the wretch taken?' When the police officers confirmed that Maria was in custody, he commented, 'Thank God: I am glad of it; that will save my life. She is the guilty party; I am as innocent as a lamb'. Although later acknowledging that he dealt the final deathblow, Manning continued to protest his innocence; despite his admission that he had repeatedly smashed the victim's skull with a crowbar he bizarrely told his brother Edmund 'I never hurt a hair of his head'.

The 'Bermondsey Murder' had attracted blanket coverage in the newspapers and the trial was eagerly awaited by the British public. The proceedings opened at the Old Bailey on Thursday 25 October and lasted two days. The prisoners did not help their cause by attempting to accuse each other for O'Connor's death. In his summing up, defence counsel for the husband conceded that he was to adopt a line that was 'odious' but he hoped to convince the jury that in this case a woman had made her husband a 'dupe' and now sought to save herself by his destruction. She was wicked and quite capable of murder. Defence counsel for Maria condemned his learned friend for the way his client had tried to blacken the name of a woman and in reply attempted

The victim Patrick O'Connor

to demonstrate that having been ill-treated by her husband, she had turned to her long-time admirer O'Connor, and was not likely to murder someone for property she could easily have obtained by 'other means'.

The jury retired and within forty-five minutes had no difficulty in returning a verdict of 'Guilty against both prisoners'. When asked if there was anything the prisoners would like to say before sentence was pronounced, Frederick declined leaving centre stage to Maria who accepted the opportunity to make an impassioned plea from the dock: 'Mr O'Connor was more to me than my husband. ... He wanted to marry me, and I ought to have been married to him. I have letters which would prove his respect and regard; and I think, considering that I am a woman and alone, that I have to fight against my husband's statements, that I have to fight against the prosecutors, and that even the Judge is against me – I think that I am not treated like a Christian, but like a wild beast of the forest'.

Unimpressed by this tirade, Mr Justice Cresswell, proceeded to don the black cap and summarily pass sentence of death commenting: 'Murder ...is at all times a horrible offence, but the present murder is one of the most cold-blooded and deliberately calculated I ever remember ... It is one of the most appalling instances of human wickedness which the annals of this court can furnish'.

Once in the condemned cells, the warring couple continued to blame each other for their plight. In a letter to Frederick, Maria refused his requests for a meeting until he agreed to state in writing that she was innocent suggesting a plot from her fertile imagination, 'You know that the young man from Jersey who was smoking in the back parlour committed the murder, and that I was from home when it was committed'. In retaliation, Frederick made allegations about Maria reported in the *Times*. 'The miserable man perseveres in his assertion that his wife committed the murder, and threatened to take his life also unless he became her accomplice'. While the culprits were on the run the same newspaper revealed that Manning was 'a discharged railway servant, who was dismissed by the directors of the Great Western Railway Company some time ago for being concerned with Nightingale and others in committing a series of robberies on that line'. With the prisoner facing the death penalty it became clear that the prisoner was prepared to make some disclosures 'with reference to some robberies in which he has been concerned' to form the basis of an 'application ... to grant him a respite'.

The Home Secretary dismissed the appeals from the bickering Mannings. Reconciled to their fate they tenderly kissed and made up in

The execution of Maria and Frederick Manning

the chapel on the day they were to face their final judgement. Hangman William Calcraft was chosen to officiate at the first execution of a husband and wife since 1700. Charles Dickens witnessed his handiwork at the public execution at Horsemonger Lane Gaol. A supporter of capital punishment although bitterly opposed to public executions, the distinguished writer was one of London's fashionable set who had paid up to ten guineas to rent houses offering a good view of the scaffold. This class of people were nothing more than obscene voyeurs with ladies using opera glasses as they would if attending a play on the London stage; yet, the author with a social conscience, who was to use Maria Manning as the basis for the character of murderess Mademoiselle Hortense in his classic novel *Bleak House*, directed his disgust at the carnival atmosphere amongst the poor 'ruffians and vagabonds' clearly enjoying the rare treat of a double hanging. The event was attended by an immense crowd of 50,000, attracting street hawkers and entertainers, pickpockets and prostitutes, all plying their trade, while people waited patiently for the main attraction, passing the time by reading souvenirs commemorating the crime and singing parodies of 'negro melodies', for example, substituting the phrase 'Oh Mrs Manning' for 'Oh Susannah'. The execution took place at 9am on Tuesday 13 November but the festivities outside the prison had commenced the previous evening. Dickens arrived upon the scene at midnight and observed in a letter to the *Times*:

When the sun rose brightly – as it did – it gilded the faces of thousands upon thousands of upturned faces, so inexpressively odious in their brutal mirth of callousness, that a man had cause to feel ashamed of the shape he wore, and to shrink from himself, as fashioned in the image of the Devil. When the two miserable creatures who attracted all this ghastly sight about them were turned quivering into the air, there was no more emotion, no more pity, no more thought that two immortal souls had gone to judgement, no more restraint in any of the previous obscenities, than if the name of Christ had never been heard in the world.

Earlier that year, the Mannings had avoided arrest after being interrogated by the police about their knowledge of the Great Western Railway robbery, but their relief had been short-lived as justice finally caught up with them over far more serious charges. When the death penalty was carried out on Frederick Manning, Henry Poole was enduring the rigours of convict life in Australia and could not conduct his duties as co-executor of his friend's will, while the chief beneficiary, Maria Manning, was in no position to receive her pitiful bequest. The whole sorry affair was summed up with an unintended railway pun contained in a verse from a poem published on a popular broadsheet entitled *The Bermondsey Tragedy:*

> *The end of poor O'Connor will long in memory reign,*
> *And shew the vice and folly which followed in its train.*
> *Oh! may it thus a warning prove to shun bad company;*
> *Never like the Mannings commit such a tragedy.*

EXECUTION EXCURSION
'Hurry my dear, we'll be late for the raising of the black flag.'

5
The Men Who Did Not Hang

Two Victorian South Devon murder cases had remarkable similarities. In 1884, John Lee committed the Babbacombe Murder and in 1896, Harry Grant was responsible for the Newton Tragedy. Both men had been invalided out of the Royal Navy and were former GWR employees. They also had a previous criminal conviction before killing a woman for whom they were each sentenced to death. Pleas of insanity were submitted on behalf of Lee and Grant who both protested their innocence yet, expressed their hope to die before escaping the death penalty in peculiar circumstances.

John Lee was born in the village of Abbotskerswell situated midway between the seaside resort of Torquay and the railway town of Newton Abbot. He joined the navy in 1879 and received an award, the Admiralty prize for general progress, whilst on the training ship HMS *Implacable* based at Devonport, Plymouth. However, his chosen career was ended by a serious bout of pneumonia and he was invalided out of the service in 1882.

Despondently returning to South Devon he gained employment as 'boots' at The Royal Yacht Hotel situated alongside the GWR station at Kingswear. Unimpressed with his prospects cleaning footwear, he obtained a position of porter on the nearby railway before being transferred to the goods yard at Torre Station, Torquay.

Royal Yacht Hotel (extreme left) alongside the railway at Kingswear

The GWR employee then made a disastrous career move, accepting the position of footman to Colonel Brownlow at his Torquay villa Ridgehill. Wealthy spinster Emma Keyse, for whom Lee had worked as the 'boy' before joining the navy, arranged the interview. She thought highly of Lee but her faith was shaken when he stole several items of silver from his new master and was arrested attempting to pawn them in Devonport. Serving six months hard labour in Exeter Prison, Lee was given a chance to redeem his character when Miss Keyse offered him employment upon his release on New Year's Day 1884. She owned a large estate in Babbacombe and resided at The Glen, a fine villa on the beach where she had received visits from three future monarchs: Queen Victoria, George V and Edward VII. Another famous acquaintance was Isambard Kingdom Brunel who bought land in the area whilst building the South Devon Railway and involved himself closely in local affairs. Emma Keyse worshipped at St Marychurch Parish Church where Brunel met the cost of a new church organ and made a generous donation to the building of a new spire. In 1854, he performed a tremendous service for the community when he lead a successful campaign to foil a plan to despoil the environment with the positioning of a Gas Works near the home of Miss Keyse

The Glen (to the right of the two trees) on Babbacombe Beach

on Babbacombe Beach. This idyllic spot was featured in *The Great Western Illustrated Railway Guide* of the period:

This charming seaside retreat is more easily reached from the Torre Station rather than that at Torquay. From Babbacombe Downs, where the best houses are to be found, one of the most delightful of the delightful views in South Devon is to be found. The eyes wander along the eastern coast to Teignmouth, Starcross, over the Exe to Exmouth, and past this point to those of Budleigh Salterton and Sidmouth. The rich dark red of the rocks, the deep tone of the sea, and the brilliant green of the meadows topping the undulating cliffs form, with the vast expanse of the sky, a most lovely panorama. Below, lies the well-sheltered beach, whence our view, looking eastward, is taken. Here the waters are clear as crystal, and splash over an expanse of such well-rounded pebbles, that the bather is guaranteed from injury. ... Babbacombe possesses the advantage of being rural and retired, while it is only a drive of two or three miles over a road (which is a perfect avenue of fine trees), and by the sea-wall, into charming Torquay. The walks east and west over the downs are unparalleled. Indeed, Babbacombe, with its lofty rocks, its beetling cliffs, and its masses of deep shadowy foliage, is a place to be remembered.

Sadly, Babbacombe was to become 'a place to be remembered' for a very different reason following the brutal death of Emma Keyse, the victim of a seemingly motiveless murder.

In the early hours of the morning on Saturday 15 November 1884, local fishermen and coastguardsmen were urgently summoned to The Glen to fight a fire that was sweeping through the house. When the flames were quelled, the smouldering body of Miss Keyse was found on the floor in the lounge, but it soon became evident that she had been killed earlier with blows to the head dealt by a blunt instrument. Also, every drop of blood had drained from her body when her throat was cut through to the vertebrae with a knife. The police investigation conducted by Sergeant Abraham Nott discovered no signs of a break-in and after questioning the victim's three female servants; suspicion soon fell on 'the only man in the house' – John Lee. The twenty year old general servant slept on a pull-down bed in the pantry only nine feet from where the victim had been attacked and the murderer would have had to squeeze past the end of the bed to reach the paraffin which had been used to start the blaze. His claim that he was a heavy sleeper and had heard nothing was disbelieved and the fact that he had been discontent and involved in heated arguments with his employer led to his arrest.

Lee's half-sister Elizabeth Harris was the cook at The Glen and gave a damning statement that Lee had been angry about receiving a reduction in his wages and threatened to have his revenge. She alleged that once, when his work was criticised, he threatened to 'push the old lady off a cliff', while on another occasion he vowed to 'level the place to ashes' and watch it burn from the top of the hill. However, it became apparent that unmarried Elizabeth Harris had been concealing a dark secret from Miss Keyse. At the time of the murder she was carrying a child. As she travelled from Torquay to give evidence at Exeter Assizes her condition was plainly visible and attracted the attention of a reporter from the *Torquay Times*:

There was quite a busy scene at Torre Station this morning owing to the number of passengers who were awaiting the arrival of the first up-train. The majority were composed of the witnesses in the case of John Lee, charged with the murder of Miss Emma Ann Whitehead Keyse, at Babbacombe. Wet weather made the circumstances very disagreeable for those who had to walk to the railway station. The coastguard officer and his men were amongst the first comers, and they were soon followed by the police witnesses. Sergeant Nott of St. Marychurch had charge of the females, notably Elizabeth Harris, half-sister of Lee, who was dressed in dark clothing, but not in conventional mourning. She appeared in fairly good health and spirits, and talked gaily with her companions while in the station. The train from Dartmouth had a large number of passengers in it before it reached Torre Station, and when all waiting there had got in, the carriages were unpleasantly crowded. Sergeant Nott rode with Harris and some of the other women. ... It will be easily understood that the general public who were in the train and those at the various stations en route, who had got information that the witnesses in the notorious murder case were near at hand, did their best to get a glimpse of them; they got little satisfaction, however, for the parties were so mixed up with the ordinary passengers that they could not be distinguished from them. There was no allusion made to the prisoner or his crime in the carriage in which Harris was seated. Her demeanour did not justify the reports which have been circulated as to her depressed condition of mind. She was silent, however, for nearly the whole time of the journey, and did nothing but look contemplatively out of the window or glance askance at a reporter in the corner of the carriage as though she suspected she was the subject of his notes.

At the murder trial held at Exeter Castle, some thirty witness's appeared for the prosecution while the accused man's only defence came in the summing up by his counsel in which he submitted the unsubstantiated theory that Elizabeth Harris may have been visited by her unknown lover on the night of the crime. Oddly, defence counsel had made no attempt to elicit the father's name in cross-examination. The jury took little more than half-an-hour to return a verdict of 'Guilty of Murder'. The Judge, Mr Justice Manisty, donned the black cap and in passing sentence of death commented on the prisoner's calm demeanour during the proceedings then concluded: 'You have been found guilty of a crime as barbarous as was ever committed. … You say you are innocent: I wish I could believe it'. At this point, the prisoner stunned the court by leaning forward in the dock and replying: 'My Lord, the reason why I am so calm is because I trust in my Lord, who knows I am innocent'.

Following Lee's arrest, the *Torquay Times* reported: 'It is said that the young fellow in custody has of late manifested signs of not being quite right in the mind'. It went on to comment, 'There is a peculiarity about the eyes; they lack lustre and expression, and are such as may be met with in our lunatic asylums'. Lee's parents also revealed that he had often acted in the past 'as though he was not right'. The foreman of the jury expressed a personal opinion to the press that, had the defendant pleaded insanity, the verdict returned would have been very different. As a last resort, an unsuccessful petition was organised asking the Home Secretary, Sir William Harcourt, to reprieve Lee on the grounds of his youth and an unsound mind. Lee's mother went to see her son for the last time before the appointed execution and found him to be totally unconcerned about his fate, cheerful, and behaving, she said, 'as if he were going to a theatre'. This was an apt description of the farcical drama that was to be played out on Monday 23 February 1885, the most infamous date in the history of capital punishment.

On the day in question, anxious officials assembled nervously on the scaffold at Exeter Prison. It was their painful duty to witness the execution of John Lee, and more than one had fortified himself with a drop of courage, although nothing could have prepared them for the harrowing scenes that were to follow. The executioner, James Berry, quickly pinioned the condemned man, drew a white cap over his head, and then tightened the noose around his neck. 'Have you anything to say?' he whispered. 'No', came the firm reply, 'Drop away'!

The hangman hesitated while the Prison Chaplin concluded the service from the Burial of the Dead: 'Now is the Christ risen from the dead...'

At the appropriate moment, Berry pulled a lever to activate the 'drop', then gasped in amazement as the trap door merely sagged two inches, leaving the prisoner precariously suspended between life and death! 'Quick stamp on it'! He shouted to the warders.

Distressing scenes followed as desperate efforts were made to force the trap open. Warders virtually jumped on the doors and risked falling into the pit with the prisoner had they been successful, but after several minutes, the bewildered prisoner was led to one side, while the apparatus was tested and found to work perfectly. Visibly shaken, Berry made a second attempt, but to no avail. Heaving with all his might, he succeeded only in bending the lever. 'This is terrible, 'cried the anguished Governor. 'Take the prisoner away!'

An artisan warder was summoned to diagnose the problem and a saw passed around the frame of the trapdoors to relieve possible pressure on the wooden boards, swollen by overnight rain. Satisfied that the fault had now been remedied, the Governor recalled the prisoner to face his ordeal for a third time. The witnesses were in a great state of shock and the Chaplain trembled as he read a passage from the service, 'The last enemy to be destroyed is death.'

Perspiring freely, Berry grasped the lever with both hands, determined that this time, John Lee would keep his appointment in Hell! The bolt was drawn and the scaffold shuddered. 'Is it all over?' pleaded the Chaplain, afraid to look. 'In God's name, put a stop to this!' exclaimed Mr Caird, the surgeon. 'You may experiment as much as you like on a sack of flour, but you shall not experiment on this man any longer'.

The Reverend Pitkin opened his eyes and almost collapsed when he realised that Lee had survived a third attempt on his life. He immediately informed the Under-Sheriff, Henry James, 'I cannot carry on!'

Without the presence of a Chaplin to sign the death certificate, the execution could not continue, therefore it was agreed to postpone the proceedings pending instructions from the Home Secretary.

John Lee was returned to his cell, seemingly unaffected by his torment, but reacted angrily when Berry came in to remove his bonds. 'Don't do that', he protested, 'I want to be hung!' 'Have no fear, 'reassured the Chaplain, with tears in his eyes, 'By the laws of England they cannot put you on the scaffold again!'

Lee recovered his composure, then suddenly remembered an extraordinary occurrence, which he had recounted earlier that morning to two warders: 'I saw it all in a dream! I was led down to the scaffold and it would not work – after three attempts, they brought me back to my cell!'

The Reverend Pitkin's assurance to Lee that he was legally protected from having to face the death penalty again was misinformed. However, the Home Secretary was empowered to commute the sentence on human-itarian grounds if he felt it appropriate. Lee's agonising experience brought about a wave of public sympathy and indignation typified by Queen Victoria who reacted strongly in favour of Lee, even though she had been personally acquainted with the murder victim. She made her feelings known in a telegram to the Home Secretary: 'I am horrified at the disgraceful scenes at Exeter at Lee's execution. Surely Lee cannot now be executed. It would be too cruel. Imprisonment for life seems the only alternative'.

Sir William Harcourt concurred and told a packed House of Commons, 'It would shock the feelings of everyone if a man had twice to pay the pangs of imminent death.'

Although an official report concluded that the scaffold had failed due to a simple mechanical fault, the findings were not made public and many people believed God had acted to save an innocent man. After serving the usual period of life imprisonment, rumours of Lee's imminent release were rife but proved unfounded and the general disappointment was recorded by the *News of the World,* 29 January 1905: 'Despite the fact that John Lee, the Babbacombe murderer, who survived three attempted executions, has completed his twentieth year of imprisonment, he was not released from Portland Prison. His release was generally expected in the district, and large crowds assembled at Weymouth Railway Station to meet the Portland trains, and more than one unfortunate man was mis-taken for the convict. But Lee himself did not arrive'.

When he was eventually released, Lee was escorted home by a warder and their arrival at Newton Abbot railway station was shrouded in secrecy. Soon a posse of reporters were on the scent, elevating the former convict to celebrity status. Lee sold his life story to the highest bidder and established a different reputation as a 'lady killer' receiving several pro-posals of marriage before choosing a bride. The wedding took place on 22 January 1909 and was reported in the *Torquay Directory:*

John Lee ... was married, by special licence at Newton Abbot on Friday. It was in December 1907, that, after serving twenty-two years in prison, Lee was released from Portland gaol. He at once proceeded to the home of his mother at Abbotskerswell, and there he has continued to reside. His visits to Torquay were frequent. More frequent have been his journeys from the village of Abbotskerswell to Newton Abbot, especially since he began to woo a Miss Bulled, who for four or five years has been the chief mental atten-dant in the female wards in Newton Workhouse. The courtship of the twain was not a secret, but secret was the date they fixed for their marriage. ...

Miss Bulled was a member of the Newton Congregational Church, and there the ceremony was conducted by the pastor on Friday morning, in the presence of the registrar, the treasurer of the church, and the caretaker. ... After the register had been signed the pastor wished the couple a happy married life, and they left the church by the main entrance, amid showers of confetti thrown by a few friends who had gathered outside. They went direct to the railway station and booked for Bristol, en route for Durham, where it is stated, they have taken a business, but they kept that a secret also, and even their closest friends cannot furnish any information as to their future place of residence.

In fact, the couple's destination was Newcastle where Lee was employed by a brewery to make personal appearances at a public house. He was extremely well paid but there was to be no 'happy ever after' for the marriage. Two years later he was filling a similar position in London at Ye Olde King's Head, Southwark, where he began an affair with barmaid Adelina Gibbs. Lee reverted to type, callously abandoning his wife without support while she was expecting their second child and emigrating to America with his new love.

John Lee –
The Man They Could Not Hang

If ill-health had not compelled Lee to leave the Royal Navy, the course of his life would have turned out very different and the same can be said of his counterpart Harry Grant, who was a plumber's mate serving on naval vessels then powered by steam. In June 1872, his world changed dramatically whilst travelling home to spend leave with his parents who ran a refreshment room in South Devon. As the train pulled out of Torre Station, one stop from his final destination of Torquay, the sailor leaned out of the carriage door, which, suddenly flew open, flinging him on to the line beneath the wheels of the carriage. He was taken to hospital suffering from serious injuries that necessitated the amputation of his left arm.

Invalided from the service with an annual pension of ten shillings (50p), the twenty-five year old naturally became depressed about his future as a handicapped person and in April 1873 he tried to shoot himself at the Burlington Arms, Chiswick. The *West London Observer* reported that Grant had been drinking heavily and struck up a conversation with an off duty policeman, PC Jennings, bemoaning his fate and embellishing the truth by telling him that he had lost his arm in a shipboard incident at Marseilles (where he served on a vessel in 1871). Stating his intention to kill himself, he shook Jennings's hand and dramatically said 'Goodbye' before leaving the pub and entering the outside lavatory, closely followed by the concerned policeman who wrenched a loaded revolver from Grant's hand. A violent struggle ensued as Jennings escorted his belligerent prisoner to the police station. Attempted suicide was then a criminal offence, but Grant was treated leniently and released from custody after a week on remand when the Hammersmith magistrates inspected his naval discharge papers which described his character as 'very good' and received a letter from the prison chaplain who formed the opinion that the incident was just a 'drunken freak'.

Even the love of a woman twelve years his junior failed to quell Grant's bouts of melancholia. In 1884, he married Sarah Daymond, the daughter of a mason from Bovey Tracey. The groom was now working as a house painter while his bride was a charwoman for two elderly sisters in Newton Abbot. The couple settled in the town, the centre of the GWR's operations in South Devon and Grant later obtained employment with the company carrying out painting jobs. Problems surfaced during the couple's tenth anniversary when Sarah became pregnant with her first child. Grant's initial happiness was permanently dispelled when he went to Newton Races, where he met an acquaintance called Mrs Barker who suggested in crude terms that he was not the father because his wife had been 'going round with other men'

Despite absolutely no evidence of his wife's infidelity, Grant chose to believe that she had been unfaithful and refused to accept the child as his own. When the baby boy was born at their terraced home in Lemon Road in September 1894, a neighbour, Catherine Massey, acted as midwife, and then had to intercede in an ugly scene as Grant saw the baby for the first time. As Sarah cradled her child, Grant grabbed a bottle and held it threateningly over mother and baby, until Mrs Massey appeared and

Harry Grant –
The One Armed Assassin

persuaded him to put the weapon down. Her husband's hatred of the child forced Sarah to arrange for a GWR engine driver and his wife, George and Susan Hales, to raise the baby from the age of six months. Although the Grants no longer shared a bedroom and the marriage was effectively over, the couple continued to live together. The relationship deteriorated even further with both parties often heard locked in slanging matches addressing each other in foul language. Sarah also became the subject of domestic violence and was once forced to leap from a window to escape from her knife-wielding husband. On another occasion, Catherine Massy was present when Grant insisted that the child was not his and that his wife walked the streets every night. Mrs Massey asked Grant, 'Have you seen her with any men?' He replied 'No'. Grant then used threatening language, 'I'll knock her brains out, that's what I'll do with the cow'. Mrs Grant retorted, 'No you won't; I'll call a policeman'. To this Grant replied, 'But I'll do it quietly'. 'Then', said Mrs Grant, 'You'll be hung'. 'No, I won't', he responded, 'for I'll finish myself at the same time'.

Why Sarah Grant chose to stay with her husband in such a hostile atmosphere is a mystery, but there was little surprise among the residents of Lemon Road at the shocking final outcome that was labelled 'The Newton Tragedy'.

On Sunday 9 August 1896, Grant left his home shortly before 8am and walked to the railway station. A month earlier he had been dismissed from his job by the GWR who were laying men off, although in Grant's case their decision had apparently been influenced by his 'intemperance'. In preparation for a ghastly episode Grant then asked William White, the landlord of the Devon Arms, to witness a will leaving all his possessions to the children of his married sister Jane Zaple. The unemployed painter

Newton Abbot Railway Station where Grant tried to commit suicide

then acted upon his constant threats to 'do away' with himself and his wife. Suicide was his intention as the 8.30am GWR 'bathing train' left Newton for Dawlish. Engine driver William Coleman, on the opposite line, spotted Grant jump off the platform and place his head on the track in front of the advancing train. He blew his alarm whistle and shouted frantically to warn driver George Harry of the imminent danger. The locomotive was immediately put into reverse to slow the train and the lifeguard attached to the front of the engine did its work and pushed the body off the track. Once again Grant had failed in his intention to die. He suffered scalp wounds and bruising to his ribs and chest but ironically the worst injury incurred was to his one remaining arm. The elbow joint was terribly mangled and crushed rendering the arm useless. The patient was rushed to hospital but refused to give the surgeon permission to amputate the limb, as he 'did not care whether he lived or died'.

Railway labourer and member of St John's Ambulance Association Harry Shephard rendered first aid to Grant and assisted in conveying him to the Cottage Hospital before accompanying two policemen to Lemon Road to inform Mrs Grant about the incident involving her husband. Concern about her welfare had also been raised, as she had not turned up for work at the home of her long standing employers, the Misses Smale. The grisly scene that awaited them was graphically described by Mr Shephard to a reporter of the *East & South Devon Advertiser*:

The door of the house ... was found locked, and no one responded to our enquiries. A ladder was then obtained, and I entered the bedroom, which is in the front of the house, accompanied by the police. On our entry, I noticed Mrs Grant lying on the floor, partly on her left side and partly on her stomach. ... I examined her and found her pulse was beating and then I lifted her, with assistance, on to the bed. ... There was a scalp wound on the right side of the head, above the right ear and the brains were protruding. On the top of the head, over the forehead, there was a nasty cut and another cut down from the ear down to the bridge of the nose, which wound was two inches in length. There was another wound over the left eye, and cut in the same way and about the same length. All of the wounds were of a very deep nature and reached the bone. The position of the body was thus: Her head and shoulders were under the bed, and her legs and lower extremities outside. She had on her chemise and stockings. I also saw a hammer lying on a table by the fireplace smothered with hair and blood.

Despite her agonising injuries, with horrific skull fractures caused by six hammer blows to the head, Sarah Grant survived a further two days

before death ended her suffering. She occasionally regained conscious-
ness but was unable to communicate and thereby shed any light on the
incident. A policeman had observed Harry Grant staggering home drunk
from the Railway Hotel on the evening of the brutal attack and neighbours had heard the couple rowing at midnight. Grant denied culpability
but was charged with murder and his trial was held at Exeter Castle on
Monday 16 November. The prosecution submitted that 'It is impossible to
come to any conclusion but that night somewhere between 12 o'clock and
the time when he left the house ... the prisoner went to his wife's
bedroom and struck her those terrible blows with the hammer from
which she died'. Defence counsel posed two questions for the jury to consider 'One question which they would have to answer was whether it was
proved that the prisoner struck the blow, and the second question would
be, assuming prisoner did so, whether he was in the condition of mind at
the time of doing it, that he was able to understand the nature of the acts
of which he was guilty, or whether he had been suffering from mental
disease in such a manner as to deprive him of the control which the mind
exercised in sane people over the acts they committed'.

In evidence, Grant's sister Jane Zaple had given details of their family
history stating that both their mother and grandmother had suffered from
insanity in extreme old age. Her brother had always had a 'bright and
cheerful' disposition but became a 'different man' following the railway
accident, which caused him to be invalided out of the navy. Medical opin-
ions expressed in the courtroom varied as to the state of mind of the
accused and the judge, Mr Justice Wills summed up the quandary for the
jury: 'Incidents showed the man's mind was not so strong as it might be,
but did it show that when he killed his
wife he did not know he was killing a
human being and offending against the
laws of God and man?'

The jury retired and took only a
quarter-of-an-hour to return a verdict of
'Guilty, with a recommendation to
mercy'. The judge assumed the black
cap and passed sentence of death commenting: 'The jury have returned the
only verdict which it seems to me they,
as honest men could do. That you killed
this woman in this cruel way there
could be no doubt. They have accompanied the verdict with a recommendation

'armless Harry Grant in the Dock

to mercy. That will be forwarded to the Secretary of State'.

The execution was set for Wednesday 9 December and in his devout ministrations with Exeter Prison chaplain, the Reverend John Pitkin, the condemned man was said 'to view his approaching end with cheerfulness' and 'has no desire that the efforts being made to save his life shall be successful'. However, following an appeal submitted by his solicitor Frederick Carter, the Home Secretary, Sir Matthew White Ridley, granted a reprieve to the prisoner despite the absence of any petition organised by even his family or friends. As the *East & South Devon Advertiser* observed: 'In Newton Abbot where the prisoner was best known, the respite occasioned some surprise. … The public were unusually indifferent … not the slightest move was made to save the man's life. The feeling in the town was altogether the other way'. The newspaper also commented that as the prisoner was 'probably as sane as most people at large' and not eligible to join the lunatic inmates of Broadmoor, his disabilities rendered him incapable of the 'hard labour' duties demanded of prisoners: 'There is naturally much speculation about what will be done with the convict. If he is sent to penal servitude he will never be able to work. He will always have to be waited on and dressed and fed like a child, as it is almost certain that he will never regain the use of his arm. … It is a curious case, and probably one of the most difficult the convict authorities have ever had to deal with'.

John Lee had earned the sobriquet 'The Man They Could Not Hang' – while Harry Grant was certainly 'The Man They *Would* Not Hang'. His fervent wish to die had been denied by the Secretary of State and his disability certainly rendered him incapable of ending his life by 'his own hand'. For Harry Grant, clemency was probably a greater punishment than execution. After periods of imprisonment at Parkhurst and Maidstone he was released after serving nearly fifteen years in March 1911. What then became of him is not known. Aged sixty-five, the helpless elderly murderer could only hope that there was a surviving member of his family to offer him a home and save him from spending the rest of his days in the Workhouse.

KEEP OUT THE COLD
If your train is not heated obtain plenty of foot warmers.
Sit on one, put your feet on another, place a couple at your back,
pop one on your lap, and you'll weather the journey like hot coals.

Great Blizzards and Great Escapes

The Great Blizzard of 1891 was the worst snowstorm experienced in England for fifty years. Freezing temperatures, unprecedented snowfalls and hurricane force gales took its toll with impassable roads, damaged property and pitiful tales of people found frozen to death in the snow. Yet, despite the sufferings of the population at large, the press reserved most of its coverage for the railway system, which was paralysed for a week. Still fresh in people's memories was the Great Blizzard of 1881, but even that terrible experience had not prepared the railroad companies for the severity of the weather that followed ten years later. The situation was summed up by the *Illustrated London News:* 'No such privations have ever been experienced in railway travel in this country within living memory ... no one could have believed it possible that in the middle of March in England people could be snowed up in trains, and in desperate peril for their lives'.

The South West region was hardest hit by the blizzard. Irate travellers gave critical interviews about long delayed journeys in snowbound carriages although their ordeals were minor compared to the lot of twelve hundred GWR labourers ordered not to return to their homes until the line was cleared all the way from Bristol to Penzance. In conditions so cold that the snow froze on their clothes encasing them in ice, they accomplished their arduous and dangerous mission with only one fatality that occurred on the Plymouth to Totnes line. Snowploughs working from opposite ends at Plympton and Kingsbridge gradually forced their way through twenty-foot drifts in which five trains were embedded. The two breakdown gangs met at Ivybridge and had just succeeded in hoisting an engine back on to the metals when a relief train from Plymouth came around a bend at 25mph and crashed into a stationary carriage of the snowed-up train. Two workmen were seriously injured in the collision and William Stentiford, a recently married Plymouth man, lost his life.

With telegraph poles blown down, communication with Cornwall was almost non-existent for several days before grim stories emerged about trains embedded in gigantic snowdrifts. The train which left Plymouth at 5pm on Monday 9 March was due at Penzance at 8.45, although it did not reach its destination until 11pm. The 'Flying Dutchman' service from London, due at Penzance at 9pm, did not arrive at all. A breakdown gang set out from Penzance in search of the express and were forced to proceed with great difficulty taking nine hours to accomplish a journey of only thirteen miles to Camborne. There they discovered the missing train had foundered when the blizzard was at its height. The 'Flying Dutchman' hauled by the locomotive *Leopard* had left Redruth one-and-a-half hours late at 10pm and the gale was driving with such force that slow progress was made beyond Carn Brae before the train ran off the snow-covered

The Flying Dutchman *off the rails at* Camborne

track within sight of Camborne Station. Five ladies on board were accommodated at the stationmaster's house while about twenty male passengers were afforded rooms at local hotels.

The Penzance to London mail train due at Plymouth at 8.10 on Monday night did not arrive at Millbay until 9.30 the following morning. With seventy passengers, including a honeymoon couple and mothers with four babies, the mail was running late and found the way ahead obstructed at St Germans. While the stationmaster Mr Priest lit welcoming fires in the waiting rooms for the comfort of the passengers and arranged for refreshments to be delivered from the village, two GWR officials who had been travelling on the train braved the elements and walked to Saltash, then on to Camel's Head to summon help. A breakdown train slowly but surely cleared the blocked line of snowdrifts, fallen trees and telegraph poles before the passengers were able to resume their journey after spending ten hours at St Germans. It would be midnight on Wednesday before the mail could be safely despatched on to London.

A train which set off from Helston for Praze with just one passenger on Monday evening at 7.40 soon became embedded in fifteen feet of snow at Crebbor Cutting. Guard Lindsey jumped out of his van and thought he had fallen down a shaft when he found himself buried up to his neck in snow. He told the story of an uncomfortable night to the *Western Morning News*:

How I got out I don't know, but after some difficulty I got to the engine, which was at this time almost covered with snow on the side from which the wind was blowing. We then tried to clear away the snow with shovels and to move her (the engine) with pinch-bars, but very soon found this an impossibility, and gave it all up. I then went down to the tail of the train and there I found the snow was up over more like a great wave than anything else, all this having gathered up since the train came to a stop. It was therefore certain that we could not move either forward or backward, and there was nothing to be done except to try and make ourselves comfortable for the night ... James Cole, the driver, Frank Webb, the fireman, the passenger, and myself – decided to get in to the warmest compartment we could find. There we sat as close together as we could, to keep as warm as possible, until next morning, nearly "paralysed" with the cold, wet through, and with nothing to eat or drink. As we sat there the steam rising up from our wet clothes made the compartment look for all the world like a washhouse. ... At 7.15 we decided to get out and endeavour to find some farmhouse where we could obtain shelter, and after walking about for some time with the snow up to our waists we succeeded in finding a cow-house, and we stayed there for a while amongst the cows, and the warmth of even this house was very acceptable. After more reconnoitring we found Polerebbor Farm, occupied by Mr. Frederick Rowe, and here we were taken in and treated with the greatest kindness.

While great inconvenience and discomfort was caused by the blizzard on the Cornish railways, the work of clearing the lines was accomplished in less time than districts in Devon and Somerset. Newspaper editor William Wingett who, accompanied by his brother, was returning to Torquay from Bristol on Tuesday 10 March recalled a nightmare journey in the *Torquay Times*:

Never had we seen the uncomfortable and draughty station at Bristol present such a desolate and woe begone appearance as it did on Tuesday afternoon. The snow was being driven through it in dense edifying clouds, and the few porters about were exerting themselves in an endeavour to keep some portion of the platform clear, piling up the snow in mounds and ridges. A bitterly searching wind was blowing with great force through the station, post office men waiting and railway officials on duty were availing themselves of sheltering nooks, the few passengers who had the hardihood to brave so terrible a storm were huddled around the fires in the waiting rooms, the bookstalls had been closed early in the day, and the bustle and activity of this usually busy station had given way to desolation.

The Zulu, by which we were travelling, came in from London only a few minutes late, a fact which buoyed our hope that the prototype of a famous African race noted for endurance would beat the storm and land us safely in beautiful Torquay. .... Our faith in the prowess of the Zulu was somewhat shaken when the examiner of tickets came round and informed us that he doubted we would get below Exeter; though he added reassuringly "We have sent on all the trains, and none of them have come back." The train started from Bristol only about a quarter of an hour after the appointed time, and rattled along at true Great Western express speed, despite occasional drifts of snow some three of four feet deep, until we reached the junction of the Weston-super-Mare loop line. Here we suddenly pulled up. The wind was howling across the flat land between Weston bay and this point with great violence, driving the freezing snow against the windowpanes with much force. There was very little of the putting the head out of the window to inquire what was the matter. Everyone knew it was the snow, and we, in common with the rest of the Zulu's human freight, possessed ourselves in patience and waited eventualities. ... When three quarters of an hour had passed, impatience began to assert itself, and seeing a signal-

'Only one line at work, sir, a goods broken down'

man with his lantern flitting about upon the white snow like a willow-the-wisp, we ventured to open the window a little way and make an enquiry. "Only one line at work, sir, a goods broken down." This was neither comforting nor reassuring, but in a little while a pilot engine came up alongside us, and we jumped to the conclusion – how belated people do catch at straws – that it brought up "the staff." Whether it had done so or not we don't know, but this we do know that very shortly afterwards we were backed over a crossing on to the up line, upon which we proceeded cautiously, passing several luggage trains, filling up all the sidings, and the broken down "goods" which blocked the down line, alongside which a break down gang was at work, a large fire upon the embankment lighting up with a lurid glare the snow laden trees in all their picturesqueness.

And so we journeyed on until we reached Taunton, where we soon learnt that we could proceed no further, that at Burlescombe, the other side of Wellington tunnel, the line was blocked with snow to a depth variously estimated at from eight to ten feet, and that three or four down trains that had preceded us, were detained at Taunton. The snowstorm was no respecter of persons, for the Duke of Edinburgh [Prince Alfred, Admiral and Commander-in-Chief of Devonport], who had left London at 10.15, was pulled up, and with his suite had been put up at the Great Western Hotel. There was something in that, for we knew that the officials would do their level best to send on a Royal traveller, and one of the rulers of the "Queen's navee," … A good story was told by some of the travellers who were in the same train as the Duke. A drunken man-of-war's man very irate at being detained for some hours in the neighbourhood of Weston-super-Mare, got out upon the footboard of his carriage, and in language more forcible than polite, became most persistent in his demands that the train should proceed. At last his Royal Highness took notice of his disorderly conduct, and ordered him back to his carriage. Jack, not recognising his superior officer, in rather coarse and vulgar language, asked him if he could not see that he was fighting his cause as well as his own in wanting the train to get on. …

Taunton station was gorged with snow and looked as discomforting as that of Bristol, and on being assured that no further could we go, we began to enquire for a hotel. "All the hotels and most of the private houses are already full with passengers who came before you," said a policeman on the platform. We, however, remembered that we would claim the friendship of the genial proprietor of the Castle Hotel … Mr. Perkins …"We are full up," he says, "but we will get you beds out" … We were afterwards conducted to the beds that had been secured for us, and we slept soundly after our experience of the blizzard of 1891. …

After breakfast, we went to the railway station to reconnoitre … . In the waiting rooms were a number of women and children who had passed the night around the fire, and who looked wearied and wretched. … About two o'clock there came a message from the railway station to the various hotels that the 3.21 down train would run, but that passengers could not be taken below Exeter. We, however, resolved to proceed by it, and take our chance of getting on beyond Exeter, and fortunate were we in doing so, for on reaching the "Ever Faithful" city, we received the welcome intelligence that the train would proceed on to Torquay, which place we reached at 6 o'clock on Wednesday evening, or just twenty-four hours after we started from Bristol, and with an experience of a blizzard which will live in our memory for many years.

The 'Zulu' due to arrive at Plymouth at 8.55 on Monday night came to grief at Brent, one of the most exposed towns on Dartmoor. The hotels were full with contractors' men engaged to lay a new railway line and the forty stranded passengers were forced to remain on the train or sleep in the station waiting room for several days. A disgruntled commercial traveller, Mr Stumbles, complained bitterly about the uncharitable treatment they had received from the tradesmen of Brent: 'The inns charged us double price for ordinary meals, and some establishments refused to supply us at all, probably thinking that a famine was impending. We returned to the station as best we could, through the great drifts of snow, and, with such provisions as we could buy, cooking such things as bloaters in the station waiting room. Our scanty supply, I must say, was most generously supplemented from the small stores which the railway officials, such as the signalman and others, had with them'.

The *Western Morning News,* which published this story also, discovered that inflation was rife amongst the hypocritical travellers, in fact, the value of their own newspaper had increased substantially during the short period that the passengers had been cut off from the world. A copy was taken to Brent by a policeman from Totnes who braved the elements and gave it to one of the beleaguered passengers. It was later revealed that the lucky recipient then turned down an offer of £2 for exclusive ownership from a fellow traveller and instead accepted five shillings (25p) to allow him to read it for one hour.

Probably the most alarming incident experienced by passengers occurred on the normally short journey on the Dartmoor branch line from Princetown to Plymouth. Starting out at 6.20pm on Monday 9 March, the train struggled only as far as Peak Tor before pulling up with a jolt. The driver immediately alarmed the passengers by admitting 'We ought not to have started'. The fireman sustained an injury to his leg when the

The stranded train on the Princetown branch line

engine pulled up but joined the driver and guard in an unsuccessful attempt to clear the line with shovels. The guard then set out to walk to Dousland for help. The falling snow blinded him and the drifts were so deep that he could not even follow the track and one hour later he gratefully returned to the relative safety of the train. The six male and two female passengers gathered in a composite carriage of one first class, one second-class and four third-class compartments where they were to spend the first of two uncomfortable nights. A passenger later described the appalling conditions: 'The snow beat in our compartment through closed doors, ventilators, and windows, so much, that in a few minutes I had two inches of snow on my umbrella. We stuffed paper, handkerchiefs, and cloth into every hole or crevice we could find, and this remedied matters a little'.

Early next morning, driver Bulland set out in a raging snowstorm and against the odds reached Dousland. The GWR immediately despatched two men with simple fare of brandy, cocoa, bread and cake, which was delivered to the forlorn passengers at 3pm. They then spent an anxious time waiting for rescue as the wind howled and the temperatures remained bitterly cold. By now an elderly married couple were suffering from the effects of exposure. At 7am on Wednesday, the travellers awoke from a fitful sleep to find the weather had partially cleared and help was unexpectedly close at hand. The train, which, by this time, was almost completely covered in snow with drifts as high as the carriage, was discovered by Farmer Hilson of Horsford, who was out in his fields rescuing buried sheep. Unbelievably, his farmhouse was only 200 yards away from the train and he was astounded that he been totally unaware of their plight.

Gratefully swapping the cold comfort of the carriage for the hearty hospitality of the farmhouse, the passengers were soon warming up and enjoying breakfast. A railway journey had become a test of survival and they began to wonder why the train was running at all considering the Princetown stationmaster's gloomy forecast when they had sought to buy tickets two days earlier 'You can have them, but I cannot promise you will get there'.

Dartmoor Prison at Princetown had a reputation as being the most inhospitable place in which to serve time. Conditions were even worse during the blizzard and soon trouble was brewing as inmates were repeatedly fed rations of salted meat. After a week in which no fresh provisions could be delivered by train, resentment and insubordination grew to such a fever pitch that a warder was attacked and stabbed in the neck by a convict. The governor reported the worrying situation to the Home

Secretary who contacted the GWR requesting them to clear the line of snow as a matter of urgency. Fifty workmen were despatched on a train accompanied by a snowplough but the work had to abandoned near Yelverton station when faced with a 200-yard long drift. Next day eighty men set out and cut a path through the drift and made it as far as Dousland. Late in the evening of the third day of the operation, a special goods train with provisions from Plymouth finally made it to Princetown to alleviate the mood of the convicts. The most thankful people to see the train service resumed were those prisoners due for release who had been forced to accept their situation as 'boarders' until conditions improved.

The GWR Plymouth to Princetown railway, was literally the end of the line for many offenders as humorously illustrated in this extract from *The Lay of the Lagged Minstrel* by An Old Dartmoor Lag, composed in 1907:

Nine months slip by, one summer day, myself and others seven,
Handcuffed and chained, we travel down for change of air to Devon.
And lest some female gay and fair, should tempt us on the rail
To stray from virtue's narrow path, we go down by the mail.

Two convicts ensured the final leg of the journey was not completed on arrival at Plymouth on 28 January 1857. Under escort with a party of prisoners being transferred from the prison hulk *Defiance* to Dartmoor, they forced off their handcuffs and jumped from the train as it pulled up at the station and were never recaptured.

An amazing getaway from a moving train on the GWR line between Reading and Twyford occurred when a party of thirteen prisoners were being transferred from Dartmoor to Chatham Prison on Saturday 4 February 1860. Shortly after 4pm the train pulled away from Reading and was travelling at 30mph when two of the convicts, John Brown and Robert Bevill, slipped free of their shackles and blindly leapt through the window of the door in their compartment. The Reading police were

Dartmoor Prison

informed by telegraph from Slough Station and a search made of the woods and thickets between Reading and Maidenhead where the escapees successfully camouflaged themselves for the night by covering themselves with tree branches.

The next day they broke into a cottage at Woodley and stole some women's hats, blouses and smock frocks, which they put on over their prison uniforms. Wearing this strange garb they strode into Reading town centre on Sunday night and immediately alerted the suspicions of a passer-by who summoned the police. Two inspectors approached the pair and when challenged Bevill immediately gave himself up but Brown swore he would not be taken and put up a violent struggle before being overpowered. Next day in court, Brown laughed heartily when the police officer, sporting a black-eye received in the struggle to arrest him, described the prisoner's bizarre disguise to the magistrates. The humour of the situation was not shared by the governor of Dartmoor Prison who took disciplinary action against two warders who had allowed the convicts to escape from their charge; an assistant-warder was dismissed from the service and a principal warder reduced in rank for negligence of duty.

A prison mutiny occurred at Wormwood Scrubs on Saturday 19 December 1891 when thirty inmates made a break during a chapel service. The ringleader was the only one to elude the warders and managed to cross the prison yard before being apprehended as he attempted to scale the outer wall. After Christmas the disorderly convicts were transferred to other prisons and a number of them bound for Dartmoor again caused trouble. They became rebellious in the train on the line between Yelverton and Princetown and details of the perilous situation were telegraphed ahead. Waiting for the insubordinate passengers at Tavistock Station was an escort of warders with loaded revolvers. With the revolt quelled, an inquiry was held and four convicts were sentenced to be flogged with the cat, whilst the chief mutineer was thrashed with the birch.

Dartmoor prisoners on the run had many obstacles to overcome; the grim weather; swirling mists that could envelope the landscape and reduce visibility to zero in seconds; treacherous moor-land bogs where many 'successful' escapers may have been sucked; sharp-eyed local people known as 'five-pounders' eager to claim a £5 reward for apprehending a fleeing villain. Fugitives also risked death at the hands of their pursuers and the irony of the law of the land which protected game birds yet justified a shoot on sight policy against convicts in flight was not lost on 'An Old Dartmoor Lag':

An escaped convict takes
cover on Dartmoor

Sometimes when things are very dull, a convict makes a dash
To gain his freedom, but the guards of him soon make a hash
Lag-shooting is such a good old sport it's never out of season,
But to shoot a pheasant in July is almost worse than treason.

One such tragedy occurred at 11am on Christmas Eve 1896 when three
men made a run from a work party digging peat near the Blackabrook
River. The chief instigator was twenty-two year old William Carter, who
had been recently parted from his new bride to serve a twelve-year sentence for robbery with violence. His co-conspirators were Ralph Goodwin
and John Martin, both serving long sentences for burglary. As the mist
descended and visibility deteriorated rapidly, work was abandoned and
the armed escort ordered the party to march back to the prison. On a
signal from Carter, earth was thrown into the faces of the guards and the
trio dashed for the cover of some woodland. The fleeing Carter was cut
down by a hail of bullets and died instantly, while Martin was quickly
cornered and knocked cold with a truncheon. Meanwhile, Goodwin van-
ished into the mist and spent the rest of the day trying to put as much distance as possible between himself and Princetown. As dawn broke the
tired and hungry convict was dismayed to discover that he had travelled
in a complete circle and arrived back within sight of the prison. Tempted
to give himself up but worried he might meet the same fate as Carter, he
set out again and made good progress on Christmas Day. At one point he
was spotted by a distant search party and gave them a cheeky wave of his
hat before disappearing from view. That night he broke into two houses

at Postbridge and obtained a change of clothes. On Boxing Day, he reached Tavistock and raided another house and hungrily ate the remains of a Christmas dinner before spending the night trudging along the GWR railway track to Plymouth. Goodwin was unable to hitch a ride on a passing goods vehicle but by morning he was at Devonport. With a successful getaway within his grasp he took to the streets where his escapade immediately came to an end due to a guilt complex. He met a policeman and wished him 'Good morning' without arousing suspicion, then, when the policeman's dog ran playfully after him, he believed he had been rumbled, lost his nerve and ran off. The exhausted fugitive was chased by the officer and quickly cornered, then flashed a stolen knife at his pursuer, who calmly out-bluffed his assailant by pretending he had a gun, which he threatened, he would have no hesitation in using unless the desperate criminal gave himself up. Returning to Dartmoor, where any vestige of festive spirit had been quashed by the death of a fellow inmate, Goodwin and Martin subsequently gave evidence at the inquest of William Carter, whose untimely death caused by thirteen bullet wounds in the back, was pronounced 'Justifiable homicide'.

Despite Dartmoor being the setting for Arthur Conan Doyle's fictional *The Hound of the Baskervilles*, which attacked and killed an escaped convict, hounds were surprisingly not used to track down fugitives until 1931. On Friday 6 February of that year, two men working in the stone sheds scaled a thirty-two foot wall with the aid of a rope to which was attached a grappling hook. The fugitives were John Mullins, aged twenty-eight, a native of York serving a sentence of three years for a housebreaking offence committed in 1929. During the First World War he had served in France with his fellow escapee, John Gasken, aged thirty-one, also of

A bloodhound picks up the trail on the railway line

York, who had completed only six months of a five year sentence for housebreaking, forgery and false pretences. While serving a previous period of incarceration in November 1921, Gasken had boldly walked out of Birmingham Prison wearing a warder's uniform.

Instead of blindly heading out across the moor in the thick fog, the duo cleverly followed a leat leading to Burrator Reservoir. The next day they stole food and a change of clothing from two unoccupied houses near the GWR railway station at Yelverton. By now, three bloodhounds loaned from kennels at Liskeard had picked up the scent and were hot on the trail but the hunt was called off after the eldest dog collapsed exhausted after five hours on the run.

On Sunday morning, Mullins was recaptured on the outskirts of Plymouth after the fugitives had become separated. Gasken remained at liberty for a further two days. During Monday, he sold a stolen jumper at a second-hand shop and bought himself a cup of tea and two pasties before spending the day at a branch library where he read about the hue and cry for his capture. He was finally apprehended near the GWR locomotive depot at Laira on the outskirts of Plymouth. Hoping to board a goods train to Bristol, he walked along the track using a stolen torch. Along the way he had spoken to some railway workers who mistakenly presumed he was a railway detective searching for the escaped convict. With the bloodhounds closing in and baying loudly in the distance, a policeman saw Gasken entering an office in the railway siding. When challenged Gasken claimed his name was Brooks and that he had just arrived from Southampton and was waiting to board a boat at Plymouth. His story was disbelieved and he was detained and questioned by a suspicious Detective-inspector Lucas: 'I believe your name is Gasken and that you are missing from your home on Dartmoor'. Still refusing to accept that the game was up Gasken replied innocently, 'Where is Dartmoor?' 'You will know soon enough' was the confident reply and after vainly protesting 'You are making the worst mistake you ever made in your life', Gasken finally dropped the pretence and admitted he was the missing convict adding 'I am hungry and fed up'.

John Gasken's five days at liberty had taken its toll on his health and he was confined in the prison hospital having developed pneumonia. After his capture he told police 'I didn't know what Dartmoor was like – I'll never try it again' yet, within two years he was on the run again. This attempt was made on Wednesday 15 November 1932 when Gasken accompanied by London burglar Frederick Amy were carrying out repairs to the roof of some cells and utilised a ladder, thoughtlessly left unsupervised for their building work, to scale a fifteen foot wall to the outside. Although never venturing more than thirty miles from the prison, Gasken and Amy established a record for escaped Dartmoor convicts and were at liberty for six days before their recapture. Neither man had been involved in the infamous Dartmoor Mutiny in January of that year when prisoners planned a mass breakout. The attempt was made and thwarted as 350 men were being escorted to a Sunday chapel service. The prisoners then went on the rampage for an hour vandalising and burning prison buildings. Many surrendered and quietly returned to their cells before the hard core rebels were finally brought under control when forty policemen drafted in from Plymouth charged with drawn batons. Security had supposedly been stepped up following this incident that attracted national headlines, so the escape of Amy and Gasken was an added embarrassment for the prison authorities.

Bloodhounds were brought from Shaugh Prior but the hunt was temporarily called off at nightfall. Meanwhile, the fugitives made their way towards the railway at Horrabridge Station and on Thursday night broke into the booking office and took oilskin coats bearing the distinctive initials GWR. The robbery was discovered at 6am and the bloodhounds soon picked up the trail and followed it along the railway line in the direction of Tavistock until the scent deviated to the moor where it was obliterated amongst a flock of sheep. Gasken and Amy laid low during the day then completed their chosen route along the GWR track to Tavistock where they joined the Southern Railway line at Lydford. Gasken realised that he would be expected to retrace his earlier escape to Plymouth, therefore had decided to try his luck in the opposite direction walking from Lydford to Exeter. Throughout the weekend the police searched in vain for the two men. According to the convicts, at one point the bloodhounds came within a few yards of their hiding place and the fugitives stroked a small terrier accompanying the search party until it ran off disinterested. Continuing their journey along the railway, they met a signalman and satisfied his curiosity by convincing him that they were seeking work. They net closed in when they broke into a house at Crediton and stole food, money and a change of clothes leaving behind the GWR oilskins. Late on Tuesday night their record-breaking escape came to an end only twelve hours short of a full seven days at liberty. Spotted on the railway track on the outskirts of Exeter, they went quietly when approached by two policemen. John Gasken was normally one of the best-behaved men in the prison but could not resist the opportunity to outwit his captors when the chance presented itself to go on the run. When asked by a policeman if he was glad his latest escapade was over he replied ominously, 'Yes, but I didn't want it to end this way'.

7

Bizarre Railway Suicides

One historic weekend in May 1892, gentlemen of the press con-
verged on railway stations to pen eulogies for the imminent
'death' of broad gauge travel. Watched by a nostalgic crowd gathered on Paddington Station, the locomotive *Great Western* had the honour
of hauling the last such train to Penzance. The emotional scene was
described by a correspondent of the *Pall Mall Gazette*:

> *Isambard Kingdom Brunel's broad gauge is dying in gallant style ... At
> 10.15 ... the stalwart driver touched the whistle, and the "Great Western"
> spoke, in one shrill cry, her echoing farewell to London ... the mighty motor
> glided serenely forth upon her final journey. As she swept out our hats were
> raised by one consent, and a lusty cheer went up and spread down the long
> platform. ... As the guard's van brought up the rear, the old guard leaned
> out and called for "one all together". The crowd responded with one mighty
> shout, and so took sorrowful leave of the last of broad gaugers'.*

The Great Western Railway Company had bowed to the inevitable and
taken the decision to fully standardise the railway network in order to cut
detrimental costs to services and remove chaos and inconvenience expe-

95

rienced by passengers at places like Gloucester where, before standardisation, everyone had to change trains when broad gauge met narrow gauge. This problem was partially solved by the introduction of 'mixed' gauge, with sections of track fitted with three lines, which allowed trains of both gauges to travel along the same route. The final nail was driven into the broad gauge coffin when five thousand navvies were despatched on special trains to strategic points along the route from Paddington to Penzance in readiness to convert the remaining 177 miles of solely broad gauge track, which necessitated the complete replacement of the line between Exeter to Truro.

In what was rightfully described by the *Torquay Directory* as 'an engineering feat, which will rank as one of the most remarkable ever executed in the history of the country' the work was completed in only thirty-one hours. Furthermore, the newspaper also affirmed that the vast workforce had emerged from the frantic weekend's activities unscathed: 'Not a single accident has occurred throughout the whole length of the line, the arrangements were of the most perfect character, the weather most favourable for the purpose, and the task accomplished without a hitch'. There had however, been a tragic incident in the week leading up to the operation. At Plymouth, the superintendent of the line, Mr Burlinson corrected an earlier statement to the *Daily News*: 'I was wrong in saying that there had been no fatality, for one of our poor fellows in Devonshire became so possessed of the subject that he went out of his mind, and in the belief that he had not tools enough to take his share of the work, he got melancholy mad and drowned himself'.

The 'poor fellow' in question was James Webber, a thirty-four year old ganger-platelayer who had been involved in the intensive preparations for the conversion. Rails and sleepers along the track were cut to length in advance to enable the imported contingent of men to carry out their task more swiftly and meet the tight deadline. Webber was responsible for a two and a quarter mile section of track near his Torquay home and had been making good progress but became increasingly anxious about prospects for the vital weekend operation. Married with three young children, he talked incessantly about the problems he faced to his wife Ellen and complained that he was suffering painful headaches caused by the pressure of work, which, he said, required a good deal of study and planning. He was also worried that insufficient equipment had been provided for the expected influx of labourers for which he was to have charge.

At the beginning of the week in which the work was to begin in earnest, Webber left for work on Monday morning accompanied by GWR labourer Alfred Underhill who was lodging with his family. After break-

Breakneck Tunnel approaching Hollacombe, Torquay

fasting with his men at Torquay Station and issuing instructions for work to be carried out by the points at Hollacombe near Torquay Gasworks, the ganger disappeared. At 11am John French was driving his cart past the gasworks to collect sand from nearby Hollacombe Beach and saw the despondent ganger walking along the railway track with his head down and his hands in his pockets. Three hours later, at low tide, the witness returned to the beach where fellow carter John Martin drew his attention to a dead man on the seashore. French was horrified to see, lodged between two rocks and entangled in seaweed, the body of the man he had seen earlier on the track. PC Clinnick was informed of the grim discovery and observed that the drowned man's pocket watch had stopped at 12.20pm.

Medical examination revealed the body had no external injuries to indicate that Webber had met with an accident or fallen into the sea off the cliffs overhanging the beach. Nor was any note found at his home or on his person to indicate that he intended to take his own life. The following day an inquest was conducted by South Devon Coroner Sydney Hacker who in his summing up stressed: 'The evidence did not seem to throw much light on exactly how the deceased came to meet his death. The pressure in his head referred to by his wife might have been a hallucination; more significantly, it was evident that his recent behaviour had undergone a change. Work colleagues had testified how he seemed deep in thought and preoccupied of late and this was accounted for by increased anxiety in connection with his job'. The jury retired and reached the painful conclusion that the deceased had simply waded into the sea and committed 'Suicide whilst suffering from temporary insanity'.

A few days later, as a group of spectators cheered a train dubbed 'The Last of the Mohicans' on it's final journey through South Devon to Kingswear and celebrated the passing of the broad gauge era with a chorus of 'Auld Lang Syne', young widow Ellen Webber was left to reflect why a loving husband and father with no financial troubles, successful in his job and highly thought of by his superiors, had become depressed to the point that he been unable to face the responsibility for an operation which, thanks in part to his preparatory input, had gone so smoothly. The changeover event was marked with reverence by the normally satirical magazine *Punch*, which published an illustration portraying the ghost of Brunel looking down on the burial of the broad gauge locomotive accompanied by a poem from Edwin Milliken whose concluding verse might also be applied to the memory of James Webber:

> *Slowly and sadly we laid him down,*
> *He had filled a great chapter in story;*
> *We sang not a dirge, we raised not a stone,*
> *But we left the Broad Gauge to his glory.*

Delays to the broad gauge operation would have inevitably occurred if James Webber had chosen to end his life by laying down on the track in front of a train – a method favoured by many people with suicidal tendencies. One particularly unfortunate case was that of a young mother who was driven to this end by fear of her brutal husband. GWR ganger John Haynes was supervising a team of labourers when he discovered the decapitated body of a young woman on the mixed gauge 'up' line of the railway bridge over the River Kennet at 10.15am on Wednesday 6 December 1871. He described the grisly scene: 'The head was about four feet from the body. There were no signs of any scuffling. The shoulders were right up against the rail and her hat was by her feet. The body appeared as if she had laid down with her face to London, the opposite way to which the train approached'.

The Punch *cartoon marking the end of Brunel's broad gauge*

Finding the decapitated body of Jane Partridge

The person who had destroyed herself was Jane Partridge, aged twenty-five. Married to Alfred Partridge, a former timber merchant of seemingly independent means, the couple had two babies aged nineteen months and three months. The family had moved from London to Reading about five months earlier and lived in the Newtown area of Reading at Orta Villas, Rupert Street, where Jane gave birth to her youngest child. Neighbours considered the Partridges to be affectionate and loving to one another until an argument broke out between the pair on Monday 4 December. Jane Partridge went to the butcher's with her children and bought some beef and mutton that she placed on the frame beneath the perambulator. When she returned home from the shops she found that the meat had fallen off and been lost. This minor incident angered her husband who had been drinking heavily. He lost his temper and struck her several times to the head, drawing blood from her mouth and she was heard to cry 'Oh, Alf, don't kill me; let me live for my baby's sake'.

The bouts of violence continued throughout the following day and were overheard by Ellen Halliday who lived next door with her mother. At an inquest held at the Dreadnought public house she told the Coroner William Weedon: 'I have been very friendly with the Partridges, sometimes sitting in their house all day long at needlework. They always appeared very happy indeed together. I last saw Jane alive on Tuesday morning. They were in the front bedroom when I first heard them quarrelling before I went into the house about ten o'clock. He seemed to be quarrelling about some beef and mutton which she had the misfortune to lose the night before. I thought he struck her then because she screamed out "Oh, Alf! Don't beat me so". I heard a great scuffling about. It seemed he pushed her down on to the bed. She said, "Oh, my poor head!" and he said, "It would not take much to smash your poor head". I went into the house to enquire what was the matter. The children were crying so, and they very seldom cried. Mrs Partridge was sitting in a chair in the same room with the children in her arms, in their night dresses and she was bleeding from the mouth. I asked her what was the matter with the children and she said, "Nothing, thank you", and she pointed to her mouth and to her husband lying on the sofa, and then she pointed to the bottle on the table which he had been drinking out of. She laid the baby in the bassinet, and put her hand up to her face, and said, "Oh, what a brute he is". I asked her if I should stay, and she said, "No, prey don't stay; he might strike you as well". Directly after I was gone he got up, and we heard him beating her again. He beat her four times during the day. Between twelve and one I went to the police station and fetched a policeman down, but just as he came down it was all quiet, so he did not stop. The disturbance continued until about five in the evening. Next morning Mr Partridge told me his wife had been out all night and asked me if I knew where she was. I said, "No, I wish I did".'

Sarah May who lived opposite the Partridge family recalled, 'At twelve o'clock on Tuesday I heard a smash, and saw Mr and Mrs Partridge at the window. He was knocking her about with his fists. He broke the window and then they moved to another room. At two o'clock I saw him knocking her about again. We saw a policeman, and he said he could not interfere. I saw nothing more 'til five. I went to my door and heard screams a little up the street. I saw Mrs Partridge running back towards their house, and he ran after her. She ran past the house. Mr Partridge went indoors and called out "Jane, where are you?"'

At 5pm, Jane had been sent out to buy some more rum for her drunken spouse. He saw her return and place the bottle of spirit on the step of the front gate before running off down the street. The enraged husband opened the door, lurched down the path and accidentally smashed the bottle by kicking it over before grabbing his wife who slipped from his grasp and got away while he thought she had gone back inside the house. Partridge roamed the streets looking for his wife and he was seen returning to the house and putting the babies to bed at 7pm. Next day he had sobered up and immediately realised what must have happened when he heard that a body had been found on the railway line. Remarkably composed after identifying the gruesome remains of his wife he agreed to give his hazy version of events at the inquest: 'There was a quarrel between us, which originated on Monday evening, owing to deceased losing things she had purchased in Reading. I was then slightly under the influence of drink. On Tuesday the disturbance was renewed. I am not certain that I knocked her about; I don't think I did. I was still under the influence of drink. She left home about five o'clock that evening to get me some spirits; she brought them to the gate, but I did not notice where she went to after that; she did not come home. About eight o'clock I enquired next door for her, but not finding her I went indoors, thinking she was either gone to London or was at a neighbour's. Next morning I made enquiries and found deceased had been found on the line and brought here'.

Any suspicion that Partridge may have caught up with his wife and killed her before placing her body on the track was dispelled by surgeon Francis Workman who determined that the deceased was run over while alive or immediately after death by other means. As Partridge had been seen returning home several hours before the incident occurred, it ruled out any suggestion of foul play. At the inquest, Dr Workman described the injuries to the deceased: 'The head was completely severed from the body just below the head. The lower jaw was also cut and injured. The teeth were clenched and the tongue was between them. The muscles of the neck torn through were partly slotted. The arms were crossed over the chest and the neck was so mangled that I could not see whether the throat might have been cut or not before the train passed over it. The hands being moderately closed there is no indication of any struggle immediately before death'.

After conferring for two or three minutes the inquest jury recorded a verdict of 'Deceased committed suicide whilst in a state of excitement, caused by the ill-treatment of her husband'.

Strangely, Alfred Partridge refused to give details of his previous address to the Coroner and it transpired that he had something to hide. Whilst living in London, he had been sentenced to fourteen days imprisonment at the Thames Police Court for wilful damage to his father-in-law's house, where his wife had taken refuge after a bout of domestic violence. Following the inquest he was arrested and charged with having unlawfully assaulted and beaten his wife. Alfred Partridge was not considered accountable for his wife's actions after his violent conduct; if aggravated assault was proved, the maximum sentence that could be imposed was six months imprisonment. Upon considering the evidence the sentence of the Reading Magistrates was that he should serve three calendar months with hard labour.

It is a sad fact that many people choose to end their lives on the railways, although there can be few instances where a person intending suicide bought a ticket before doing so. A notable exception occurred in Cornwall on Saturday 7 November 1903. As the GWR *Cornishman* express pulled into Truro Station from Penzance at 11.40am, the attention of Saturday morning travellers was drawn to a distinguished looking gentleman with a white beard, soberly attired in full mourning dress wearing a black frock coat and silk top hat. The grief-stricken passenger boarded a third class carriage with a ticket for St Austell and it was evident to casual observers that he was travelling to attend a funeral; what they did not know was that the morose gentleman was planning his own.

The man in black did not alight at his designated stop of St Austell. It was not until the train had passed through Lostwithiel that he rose from his seat and walked along the corridor. As the train emerged from a tunnel, female passengers tittered as they saw the gentleman entering the ladies toilet. Embarrassed laughter turned to murmuring indignation when the gentlemen emerged from the closet and looked nervously around before stepping back into the female domain. As the train slowed down on the approach to Bodmin Road Station, one of the shocked passengers, Leah May of Par, considered whether to confront the interloper and point out his error before a loud noise rang out and she immediately realised what had happened. She summoned Porter Pindar and told him, 'That gentleman's shot himself'. Rushing to the lavatory, they opened the door and saw the man stooping with a revolver in his hand and blood streaming from a self-inflicted head wound. Other passengers heard the report and a doctor and policeman, who happened to be travelling on the train, joined the railway guard at the scene of the atrocity and saw the body of the unfortunate man apparently positioned in front of a mirror in order to direct the weapon accurately at the middle of his forehead. He was resting on his haunches with both arms between his legs, the gun held in his right hand and his finger still on the trigger. The revolver had five chambers and a fatal one had been discharged. When removed from the train and taken to the waiting room, the body was searched and in addition to a third class railway ticket was about £5 in cash and a gold watch and chain. The only clues to his identity were a cheque for £50 and his deceased father's memorial card. The dead man's face was hideously splattered with blood but was instantly recognisable to Mr Kent, the stunned stationmaster of Bodmin Road. The suicide victim was none other than the former Mayor of Truro, Silvanus Trevail, an eminent architect responsible for the design of many distinguished buildings in Devon and Cornwall known affectionately as 'Trevail's Landmarks'.

The shock felt by the stationmaster was shared elsewhere. The disbelief that a brilliant career could come to an end in this way was summed up by the *West Briton & Cornwall Advertiser:* 'That such a strong-minded, iron-willed man as Mr Silvanus Trevail, F.R.I.B.A. [Fellow of the Royal

Institute of British Architects], should lose his mental balance, and seek self-destruction, was, indeed, a staggerer for most people'. However, it transpired that the unmarried architect had been sinking into an overwhelming pit of depression over a period of two years. In 1902, he had been deeply upset by the death of first, his mother, then his father, to whom he was particularly close. His parents were buried in the local churchyard at Luxulyan and Silvanus presented a peal of six bells to the church to commemorate their memory. Early in 1903, Trevail went for a prolonged holiday abroad for the benefit of his health but his disconsolate mood was not helped by a series of personal disappointments on his return when he failed to be re-elected as Mayor of Truro, then immediately lost the coveted position as President of the Society of Architects.

According to people who knew him well, Trevail then displayed all the classic signs of a nervous breakdown, becoming increasingly absent-minded, morose, reclusive, over-anxious and paranoid. Alfred Cornelius, his loyal assistant of many years standing went further and believed his employer to be 'thoroughly unhinged' in the days leading up to his death. The ailing architect told his cousin Charles Trevail that 'detectives' were after him and blamed this imaginary foe for 'missing' documents that were actually perfectly safe in his possession. By the medical standards of the day, perhaps Trevail's progressive illness would have made him a candidate to become an inmate of his latest project at the County Asylum in Bodmin where he was engaged to design an extension. Crisis point came in the week of Trevail's 52nd birthday when he received news of the death of a favourite uncle, retired farmer Henry Trevail. Writing a letter of sympathy to his cousin Charles in Luxulyan, which, with the benefit of hindsight gave a strong indication of his state of mind, the architect darkly stated his intention to attend the funeral on Saturday afternoon, 'if not prevented by what I am unable to control' adding 'You will, I am sure be sorry to hear that I am no better'.

When the fateful day arrived, instead of travelling on the Newquay line and changing at Par for Bridges, the nearest station to Luxulyan, Trevail bought a ticket to St Austell, but journeyed beyond that point before finally summoning up the courage to end his life at Bodmin. Relatives attending the funeral on Saturday afternoon were discreetly informed of the tragedy to befall one of the Duchy's favourite sons. As the mourners gathered to watch the cortege enter the church, the news was whispered from one to another. The *Western Morning News* noted the irony of the situation: 'While the Luxulyan ringers were ringing a peal of muffled bells for the uncle, the nephew, the giver of the bells, was lying dead at Bodmin Road'.

After serving an apprenticeship with a London architect, Trevail had returned to his native county in 1872 and quickly established an enviable reputation designing numerous public buildings including schools, hospitals, libraries, chapels, banks, as well as fine houses and commercial premises. RIBA regularly selected his works to represent the best of British architecture at exhibitions held at Paris, Sydney and Melbourne. In his native Cornwall, his greatest contribution was made to the development of tourism which was recognised as 'enhancing its attractions as a health and holiday resort to such an extent that thousands now visit the county annually, who hitherto would have gone elsewhere'. During his frequent travels to America and Europe he was impressed by the standard of hotel accommodation and realised that the development of the railroad at home would soon attract holidaymakers to the stunning coastal locations of Cornwall. Forming the Cornish Hotels Company in 1890, Trevail designed a chain of hotels including the Pendennis Hotel, Falmouth; Carbis Bay Hotel, St Ives; King Arthur's Castle Hotel, Tintagel; the Housel Bay Hotel at the Lizard; the Atlantic and Headland hotels, Newquay. During this period he formed an alliance with the London and South Western Railway encouraging them to challenge the traditional territory of the GWR who regarded Cornwall as their stronghold and opposed the plan in Parliament. The outcome was revealed in Trevail's obituary in the *Western Morning News*: 'In 1894 Mr Trevail made a great effort to bring down the second great trunk line of railway through Cornwall, and succeeded to the extent of procuring the rejection by the House of Commons of a "Blocking Bill" upon its third reading, and after it had passed the committee stage, an achievement unprecedented in Parliamentary history'.

Trevail's antipathy to the GWR is hard to reconcile as he designed the Great Western Hotel, which opened at Newquay in 1879. Had some perceived injustice led him to swap allegiance to their fiercest rivals? He was known to be a man that harboured grudges indefinitely and it may be no coincidence that he chose to end his life in a blaze of bad publicity for the GWR.

The first Great Western Hotel, which opened at Paddington in 1854, was to provide the backdrop for a dramatic sequel to a double tragedy when a man was found dead in the smoke room at 9.30pm on Saturday 15 August 1931. A member of

Great Western Hotel
NEWQUAY   (FULLY LICENSED)   CORNWALL

First-Class RESIDENTIAL HOTEL

C. V. HOOPER   -   -   -   -   Proprietor

staff at the hotel saw him collapse and he was laid on a couch before a policeman was called to the scene. Upon searching the body it was discovered that the dead man had only 2p in his possession and in his pocket was a card on which was written a cryptic message: 'If anything happens to me tell my Rose I died loving her. The brain must have snapped'.

The man, who had taken his own life by administering poison, was Arthur Aldous, aged thirty-eight, a travelling salesman who the previous day had given evidence at the inquest of his lover Ivy Cracknell, She was the wife of a policeman who had come home unexpectedly the previous Sunday and discovered her committing adultery. The enraged husband stormed into the bedroom and dragged the naked, quaking Aldous out from his hiding place under the bed. 'I set about him' said the officer, 'and gave him a good hiding. He lay in the corner like a rat, and refused to move. I made him put on his clothes, and slung him out of the house'.

A few days later Ivy Cracknell killed herself with a dose of cyanide of potassium and left an accusing suicide note: 'I hope you will find Aldous and punish him as he deserves. He gave me this stuff to take ... so now you can have him for murder'. At the inquest Aldous claimed he was in the habit of carrying poison and she must have taken the bottle from his pocket. Earlier that week Aldous himself had been arrested for threatening to commit suicide. He lived in Paddington at Victoria Street with his common-law wife Rose Patrick. She was a widow who had allowed Aldous to move in with her nine years earlier 'under a promise of marriage'. When she heard about her partner's affair she insisted that he leave her house. Aldous later returned and threatened to swallow poison on her doorstep, causing her to call the police. He was still in custody when he was taken under police escort to the opening of the inquest into the death of Ivy Cracknell and later that day appeared before the Magistrates at the South-Western Police Court where the case against him was dismissed. Earlier, the inquest had been adjourned and Arthur Aldous left the court a worried man, for if Ivy Cracknell's last words were believed then he would almost certainly face criminal proceedings for inciting someone to commit suicide.

On the day of his death Aldous attempted to patch up his rocky relationship by telephoning Rose at the office where she worked. In a desperate bid to win her back, he tried to convince her that he had only called on business at Mrs Cracknell's house in Kettering Street, Streatham. Whilst there he suffered a heart attack and she had invited him to lie on the bed and rest. PC Cracknell had then returned home, misread the situation and attacked him in a violent temper. When Rose refused to believe this ludicrous explanation she returned home that night and found two letters had been delivered by hand. One envelope contained poison crystals and the other a pathetic plea from Aldous, 'Believe me girl. Don't think so unkindly of me. Black as it looks, I am innocent. God protect you always'.

In evidence at a reconvened double inquest held on Wednesday 2 September, Rose Patrick told the Coroner that her fiancée 'had always carried poison since I knew him' and frequently threatened to kill himself. Some unintended levity was introduced into the proceedings when she revealed how she had tried to prevent the worst case scenario, 'I took it away from him on one occasion and filled the packet with sugar, and he went about with the sugar instead of poison for about two years'.

In his summing up, the Battersea Coroner, Dr Edwin Smith, firstly drew the jury's attention to the mystery surrounding the death of thirty-six year old Ivy Cracknell:

'We do not know whether Mrs Cracknell's statement that the poison in her possession was given to her by her friend Aldous was right or not, but you no doubt will have noticed that the witness with whom he had been living, Mrs Patrick, had some of the poison pushed through her letter-box and she has got the idea that he might have been suggesting that she should take her own life with this poison, which rather supports the idea that he had given it to the other woman, Mrs Cracknell'.

With regard to the peculiar habit of Arthur Aldous, whom the Coroner described as being 'an enthusiastic distributor of cyanide of potassium'. Dr Smith deduced: 'He was obviously suicidal. It might have been thought that the fear of a serious criminal charge might have precipitated his action, because he was in Court and would hear that anybody supplying poison to a person for the purpose of suicide would have to face a very serious charge, which might be as serious as murder'.

Directed by the Coroner, the jury retired and dutifully returned the predictable verdict that Ivy Kathleen Cracknell and Arthur Harston Aldous had both committed 'Suicide during temporary insanity'. Interested observers of the proceedings were legal representatives protecting the interests of the Great Western Hotel – where the finale of this tragedy had occurred – and Boots Chemists who, quite properly as the law stood at the time, had supplied Aldous with lethal amounts of cyanide of potassium. Customers were merely required to sign a register. Following his arrest outside Rose Patrick's home Aldous was searched by the police who found enough poison on his person to kill twenty people, yet he was freed by the magistrates. Attempted suicide was then a criminal offence, but as the Coroner astutely observed during his summing up at the inquest, 'Suicide was an enterprise where you were regarded as insane if you succeeded, but if you failed nobody said anything about insanity. You were regarded as sane'.

COLLISION COURSE
Old Gent: 'We seem to be going fearful fast'
Swell (checking watch): 'Yes, wouldn't be surprised if we crash at this rate'

The Norton Fitwarren Train Disasters

The GWR celebrated 'The Centenary of the Holiday Line' in 1935 and the company's annual guide *Holiday Haunts* expressed the hope that even more resorts would be made accessible during the following decade. Alas, travelling for pleasure would be positively discouraged when the rise of Nazi Germany plunged Europe into inevitable conflict. Nationalisation of the railroad system would be introduced after the Second World War during which, the government took control of Britain's four main-line railway companies; the GWR and its three competitors; the London Midland and Scottish (LMS); the Southern Railway (SR); and the London and North Eastern Railway (LNER). The 'Big Four' fulfilled a vital role in wartime and were regarded as the main artery of the nation's lifeblood transporting food, raw materials, munitions and service personnel. In this respect, the railroads became an obvious target for enemy aircraft and during hostilities; trains were regularly strafed and bombed. Although there were many human casualties of the attacks on railways, amazingly, only one locomotive was damaged beyond repair throughout the entire war.

Drivers on the GWR line to the West Country had to run the gauntlet along their route of air raids on the major cities of London, Bristol, Exeter

IS YOUR JOURNEY REALLY NECESSARY?

A wartime advert discouraging rail travel

and Plymouth. The dangers were accentuated by having to adjust to operating at night in 'black out' conditions, which were to contribute to a terrible railway disaster at Norton Fitzwarren, near Taunton.

At 4am on Sunday 4 November 1940, the GWR London to Penzance express was gliding through the darkness when a sudden impact hurled the engine and front coaches up in the air. As the train plunged off the track with wreckage scattered in all directions, many of the passengers lives were saved when they instinctively threw themselves to the floor of the carriages, believing that the area was under attack, but they were soon to discover that the derailment was a pure accident and not the result of enemy action or sabotage.

The train was carrying 900 passengers and twenty-six of them lost their lives and a further fifty-six seriously injured. Although shocked and shaken, the driver of the locomotive, Percy William Stacey, clambered clear of the engine which, was on its side alongside a stream, and waded through waist deep water before running three quarters of mile along the line to place the signals at danger and stop any oncoming trains. In the stricken locomotive lay the body of Fireman Seabridge, crushed beneath the mangled engine *King George VI*.

Awakened by the rending noise of the crash, people from Norton Fitzwarren rushed to the scene and heard the cries of entrapped passengers. Casualties were taken to the village hall until medical help arrived from Taunton. Railwaymen, troops and ARP wardens undertook the heartrending task of searching for survivors which, as the *Somerset County Herald* reported, was hampered by the blackout regulations: 'As by the meagre light of torches, all that could be used, heavy crowbars and other tools were plied to the wreckage, ambulance men pulled out the dead, the

MURDER & MYSTERY ON THE GWR

dying, and the injured, while doctors, including two naval surgeons who were on the train as passengers, performed wonders on those alive. One man had a leg amputated while he was under the wreckage. The courage and fortitude of the injured and entrapped was impressive'.

Many of the casualties were men from the Royal Navy reporting for duty at Plymouth - sailors who had seen action at sea and could hardly have expected to be killed or seriously injured travelling at home on a train. Indeed, the scene resembled the deck of a crippled battleship and there were many stories of heroism among the injured. A petty officer from Taunton, who had twice emerged unscathed from torpedoed ships, broke his leg in the rail accident. A Bristol stoker, just passed fit for duty after recovering from a shrapnel wound to the shoulder inflicted on HMS *Exeter* at the Battle of the River Plate, was rendered incapable of active service after losing several toes in the railway crash. Their courage was summed up by another poor sailor lying trapped with a shattered leg and his arm torn off who stoically told a rescuer, 'I'm all right, mate. Give me a fag'.

Two large cranes were brought up from Swindon and Newton Abbot to assist in the salvage work, by which time investigators from the Ministry of Transport were already forming the opinion that the accident had been caused by an 'unaccountable lapse' on the part of the driver. According to the official report, the 9.50pm passenger train from Paddington to Penzance passed two successive stop signals at danger and became derailed at catch points where two lines converge at the west end of Norton Fitzwarren Station.

Delayed at Temple Meads Station as bombs rained down on Bristol, the passenger train was running over an hour late by the time it reached Taunton and was switched to the relief line to allow the Paddington to Penzance newspaper train to overtake, but Percy Stacey misread the signals believing he was proceeding on the main line and continued watching a green signal intended for the newspaper train. An even worse catastrophe was narrowly avoided when the newspaper train passed the passenger train just seconds before the crash, otherwise it would have collided with the wreckage at the points where the two lines met.

Percy Stacey had a hitherto excellent record of forty years service with the GWR and frankly admitted his responsibility. In mitigation it was said that the driver's 'breakdown' could partially be explained by the strain of working in wartime conditions and the fact that a few days earlier his family had been made homeless when his house at Acton was bomb-damaged during the London Blitz.

At the opening of the inquest at Taunton, the Coroner assured relatives

109

NOTICE TO PASSENGERS

AIR RAID PRECAUTIONS

DURING AN AIR RAID :–

1. Close all windows and ventilators and pull down the blinds as a protection against flying glass.

2. If danger seems imminent, lie on the floor.

3. Never leave the train between stations unless so requested by a railway official.

4. Do not touch any outside part of a coach if a gas attack is suspected.

DURING BLACKOUT HOURS:–

1. KEEP ALL BLINDS DRAWN.

2. KEEP ALL WINDOWS SHUT except when necessary to lower them to open doors.

3. MAKE CERTAIN the train has stopped AT A PLATFORM and that you alight on the PLATFORM side.

4. WHEN LEAVING THIS COMPART-MENT, close windows, lower blinds again and close the door quickly.

These air raid procedures were posted in carriages

of the victims that the GWR accepted full liability for the crash and would deal with any claims. Driver Stacey, was formally cautioned but elected to give evidence and painfully relived the horror which had engulfed him as the train sped along buffeted by gale force winds during a misty, stormy night: 'As we moved off from Taunton I saw a green light, which I thought was mine; I am not sure of that now. I heard the siren of the automatic train control ramp just after leaving Taunton platform. I proceeded on what I thought was the main line to Norton Fitzwarren. On putting my head outside the anti-glare screen at Norton Station to see the signals for Victory crossing, I saw another train passing on my right-hand side. I immediately shut off my steam, applied my brakes, and came off the road at the catch point'.

The automatic train control (ATC) was a 'fail safe' measure to alert the driver to impending danger. When the engine ran over an electrical contact ramp in the rail, it sounded a bell in the cab for 'clear' or a siren for 'warning' – in which case the brakes were automatically applied. Stacey remembered hearing the siren but as the train proceeded without braking, he assumed the line had cleared, forgetting, doubtless due to the trauma suffered, that, at the time, he had thought it was a false alarm and used manual override to retain personal control of the brakes.

The Coroner in his address to the jury of nine Taunton men said: 'The engine driver had a difficult journey all the way from London owing to the bad weather, the mist and black-out, I think he definitely made an error. Do you think there is some excuse for the error, or do you think he has been grossly negligent? If you have any doubt in your minds you should obviously resolve it in his favour'.

The jury, who had visited the scene of the crash and viewed a scale model of the track complete with coloured signals and signal boxes, retired and after long deliberation the foreman announced their verdict:

'We find that the engine driver has been guilty of an error of judgement, but we cannot decide on the actual degree of error. It was certainly not criminal, especially in view of the abnormal weather and other conditions. It appears to us that some arrangement of communication should be made to the driver of any train entering this relief line contrary to the usual procedure'.

The finding of the inquest that Percy Stacey's actions were 'not criminal' spared him from having to face a trial for which he might have been charged with manslaughter. A GWR employee involved in similar misfortune half a century earlier at Norton Fitzwarren had not been treated so leniently; the two accidents were compared by the *Somerset County Herald* in November 1940: 'This was the worst accident in Britain for three years, and, by a strange coincidence, it occurred within about 200 yards of the last big railway disaster in West Somerset, which, also curiously enough, happened in the early hours of a November morning exactly fifty years ago –

The 1890 disaster at Norton Fitzwarren

in 1890. On that occasion ten persons were killed and several injured'.

The GWR disaster of 1890 occurred at 1.20am on Tuesday 12 November. The railway company ran Ocean 'specials' – mail trains carrying letters and passengers arriving by steamship at Millbay Docks, Plymouth. Late on Monday evening, the vessel *Norham Castle* docked from the Cape of Good Hope and forty-seven travellers were transferred to the 'Cape Mail' train. Among the passengers were a number of miners returning to their homes in the North of England and Scotland with their pockets filled with gold paid to them for their endeavours on three-year contracts in South Africa. The train departed at 12.45am and reached Exeter safely one hour later. As the train sped towards Taunton, George Rice, the signalman at Norton Fitzwarren, was to suffer an appalling lapse of memory leading to tragedy. He moved a slow moving goods train travelling from Bristol onto the 'up' line to allow an express train travelling in the same direction to pass. The experienced signalman then completely 'forgot' about the stationary slow goods train waiting near the booking office on the 'up' line, and consequently the 'Cape Mail' hurtled into it at 50mph. As a result there was a horrendous head-on collision that completely wrecked both engines and the impact piled carriages and debris to a height of thirty feet. The driver and fireman of the goods train leapt clear and rolled under a wagon, whilst the crew of the onrushing 'special' acted with great courage and stayed at their post. Scott, the driver did all he could to minimise the effect of the crash by reversing the engine and applying the brakes. Although severely injured, the crew of the mail train miraculously survived, saved by the heavy coal tender behind the engine which absorbed the impact of the crash from behind and 'telescoped' into the front carriage with terrible consequences for the occupants. Some victims were crushed and died instantly while, others lying injured and trapped, were scalded and burnt alive as steam and fire from the engine furnace swept through the carriage and engulfed the helpless victims.

While the salvage operation got underway, Scott the passenger driver and his mate were conveyed to the Devon and Exeter Hospital, while eight injured passengers were treated at Taunton and Somerset Hospital and then accommodated at the Great Western Hotel. The hotel was also utilised as a makeshift mortuary for the bodies recovered from the wreckage. Those fortunately saved had some remarkable stories to relate to the press about their survival; there was a lucky escape for a mother and her four young children – although the side of the second carriage in which they were travelling was completely smashed, Mrs Lewis, the wife of a sergeant in the 6th Dragoons, and her family were shaken but unharmed.

She felt 'Oh so thankful' to pick up her little ones alive and well after being thrown violently from their seats.

Travelling in the second compartment of the first carriage was William Geddes, a contractor with the Central Diamond Mines company in Kimberly who was returning home to Aberdeen: 'There were five of us in the compartment. I was lying on the floor of the carriage, so I did not get badly hurt. I was half asleep. Then there came a shock, but I never realised that anything had actually happened until I felt wind and rain blowing on my face. I saw people running about and began to realise that something had happened. I was squeezed in below the seats. My head was in between the axles of the carriages. I could not move my legs and they are still painful. The smoke and steam from the engine was very bad. My face was covered with blood, for two dead persons heads were squeezed so that the blood from them fell over me. The carriage formed a sort of cover for my head, and I think that saved my life'.

A travelling companion of William Geddes was Mr Wall, an electrician at the Kimberly Diamond Mines who was trapped in the wreckage for five hours. He was the only other survivor from five men travelling in the second compartment of the first carriage: 'I had just lit my pipe and was smoking, when in the twinkling of an eye, there was a smash and I felt blood running from a wound over my eye. I felt my legs jammed and felt another man jammed on the top of me. I called out for help, and heard the rescuers call out, asking me what was the matter. We heard them hacking away at the other carriages, trying to get them out, and we called out again,

Left: Mrs Lewis and her children escaped unharmed from this carriage
Right: The express train engine after being pulled away from the goods train

for the steam from the engine was choking us. It was cruel and very hot indeed. To make matters worse, the first compartment caught fire, and the smoke very nearly suffocated us. I gave up hope then and thought it must be death for all of us. My legs below the knee are badly crushed and so is my foot, but I have no bones broken. I nearly bled to death from a wound over my eye and my mouth was bruised. I was almost the last one to be rescued and during all that time I had three men on the top of me. All of our legs were mixed together. They had to get the seat away to free us'.

Ghoulish crowds gathered at the spot and had to be restrained from assembling on the track to prevent what the *Times* reported as a 'horrible spectacle' of 'people searching for bloodstained mementoes of the occurrence. ... One party of four men were playing cards at the time of the collision and they were killed outright, the cards being strewn in all directions. Most of these were bespattered with blood and were eagerly pounced upon by the more morbid of those who visited the scene'. A disapproving travelling companion of the gamblers had a fortunate escape; the Reverend Burdon, a clergyman from Dundee, travelled in the same compartment as these four men as far as Exeter. He watched their game, and, thinking they were not playing fairly, he remonstrated with them. At St. David's he left the carriage and found a seat in the next coach, a decision that saved his life. Another religious man was not so fortunate, Titus Baylis, a Negro from Kimberly who had been converted to Christianity and become a preacher in the gold fields, was decapitated in the crash. His lifeless body was carried from the wreckage some hours before his head was recovered. He

'*Ghoulish crowds gathered at the spot.*'

lost his life on his first visit to England, en route to America where he had undertaken to join a mission of the Wesleyan church.

The railway staff responded magnificently to the catastrophe. Mr Gooding, the guard of the ocean passenger mail recovered quickly from the initial shock to go to the aid of his passengers: 'The force of the collision was terrific, and I was knocked completely over in my van and very much bruised. My van was at the back of the train, which consisted of an engine, tender, two carriages and the brake. Those who were injured were mostly in the front carriage. As soon as possible I climbed on the top of the broken carriages, and commenced sawing and chopping, so as to get to the people trapped inside. I had a hand in helping them all out, both dead and living. The railway officials telegraphed Taunton and medical and other assistance, and this was not long in coming. The scene was an awful one, and the night was dark besides, while it commenced to rain hard soon after the accident happened. The cries for help were really dreadful. There was nothing unusual in the fact of the goods train being on the up line, but the signal was given "All right"'.

The man responsible for displaying the wrong signal was George Rice, aged sixty-three, who had been in the employ of the GWR for thirty-five years and had been a signalman for the past twenty-seven years at Norton Fitzwarren. He had earned six 'good conduct' stripes, each representing four years loyal service, earning a £20 gratuity for each one and a company pension but he chose not to retire because 'he did not know what he should do'. However, in January 1890, he was accidentally knocked down in the goods yard when crossing the path of a pilot engine. He suffered serious head and rib injuries requiring sustained medical treatment that kept him off work for a period of fourteen weeks. When deemed capable of resuming his duties, he worked ten-hour day and night shifts on alternate weeks. However, he often felt unwell and, as subsequent events proved, it was patently obvious that he had not fully recovered.

Sergeant Hayes of Taunton Police arrived on the scene at 3.15 and questioned the devastated signalman, 'This is a bad job. How did it happen? Rice replied, 'I had got a goods train shunting in the station yard, and I received a signal from Taunton that the fast goods train was coming. I shunted this train over on to the up line for the fast goods to pass. After the fast goods had passed through the station I received a signal that the up express was coming. I did not give it a thought about having a goods train on the up line, so I pulled off my signals, and the express came dashing on. As soon as I heard the crash I knew what I had done. If there had not been someone at the bottom of the steps when I came out of the box I should have gone over to the water and drowned myself'.

The person approaching the signal box was Charles Noble, the stunned driver of the goods train who demanded, 'What have you been doing?' Rice, suddenly realising his mistake, replied, 'Bless my heart, I have got the goods train on the main line'.

The inquest into the tragedy opened at Taunton Guildhall on Thursday 13 November conducted by the Deputy Coroner of West Somerset, Dr Cordwent. Representing the interests of the GWR was an eminent barrister and future government minister, the Hon. Alfred Lyttelton, who expressed the deep sympathy of the directors of the company for the injured and the relatives of the deceased. He reiterated that the GWR accepted in the 'fullest degree' their legal obligations for the consequences of the accident. George Rice was in police custody but agreed to testify and was totally honest in accepting the blame for the crash. After answering the barrister's questions fully, Mr Lyttelton concluded: 'Nothing will give the company greater pleasure than to relieve this poor man of any responsibility he may have incurred'.

Despite all the safeguards Rice revealed how complicated a signalman's job could be even after midnight at a countryside station. The two mainlines were mixed gauge while the sidings were narrow gauge and the signal box was at the junction of the broad gauge Minehead branch line. After going on duty at 9.15pm he had dealt with over thirty passing trains that night before fate conspired to cause a catastrophe. The sidings at Norton Fitzwarren were full of goods vehicles therefore, Charles Noble, in charge of a narrow gauge goods train shunting in the goods yard was ordered to move his train on to the 'up' line and allow the express goods to pass through on the 'down' line to Exeter. For the same reason a broad gauge pilot engine was moved on to the Minehead branch line. The express goods passed through the station and the pilot engine crossed the junction then, George Rice received a message from signal-

Left: The tender of the goods train   Right: Overturned goods truck

man Albert Allen that the ill-fated ocean mail was approaching having passed him at the Victory signal box on the Exeter side of Norton. All stations on the line between Exeter and Bristol had earlier received a telegraph 'Special ocean passenger for London hence 12.44' which was immediately acknowledged by George Rice when received at 1.04am. At 1.18am, Rice acknowledged Albert Allen's message erroneously replying 'Line clear'. Albert Allen sent a further warning 'Train on line' but receiving no answer enquired if the train had passed Norton and received the ominous telegraph message of six beats signifying 'Line blocked'. While Charles Noble and his fireman Alfred Downing were waiting on the 'up' line they placed a red light on the front of the engine as a 'danger' warning to any approaching train but replaced it with a green light after the express goods had passed in anticipation of the signalman moving them off the 'up' line. When this did not happen, Noble gave a blast on his whistle to remind Rice in his signal box about 100 yards away but got no response. If a delay occurred in such circumstances, it was the guard's duty to walk to the signal box and request the train be moved, but the guard, Mr Lowe, did not do so. Suddenly, the ocean special sped into view, the crew of the goods train had to jump for their lives as Alfred Downing shouted, 'Here is a train coming and it's not going to stop'.

Noble and Lowe both came in for strong criticism from Colonel Rich, inspector of the Board of Trade who made the following comment in his official report:

> The driver of the goods train stated that he whistled to call the signalman's attention and to intimate that he wanted to go, immediately after the broad gauge pilot engine returned on to down line about 1.19, and that he changed his head lamp from red to green about one and a half minutes before the special arrived; but as his regulations direct that he shall keep the red light exhibited so long as he is not on the proper line, I cannot understand why he changed it at the time he said he did. If he exhibited the red light, it might not only have drawn the signalman's attention to the train being on the up line, but the driver of the special would probably have observed it after he passed the up home signal when there was time to stop the special train by applying continuous braking. I consider that the driver of the goods negligence, in disregarding the company's regulations, contributed to the catastrophe. The regulations further provide that the guard of the goods train shall go himself or send his assistant to the signal cabin, and remind the signalman of the position of his train.

Nevertheless, it was George Rice who bore the burden of responsibility and when questioned about his health at the inquest he admitted that he had been forgetful since his accident in January and told the Coroner, 'I have been very well in body, but sometimes I have been queer in my head. I thought that if I went on with my work I should feel better'. He had felt unwell while on leave on Sunday. Referring to the fatal collision he said: 'I was very bad that night. I had a mind not to go on duty'.

When the inquest reached its conclusion, there was an extraordinary dispute in open court between the Coroner and the jury who attempted to deliver an unsatisfactory verdict, which did not make it clear what they considered to be the cause of the crash. Dr Cordwent tried to put the jury's thoughts into an acceptable form of words: 'The jury say that George Rice stationed at Norton Fitzwarren, and being there in charge of the railway signals and railway points did, on the early morning of November 12, feloniously and negligently ... ' At this point the Coroner was interrupted by howls of protest from the jury who objected to the expression 'felioniously' being used to describe the actions of the signal-man. Dr Cordwent pointed out that in law he could not substitute the phrase 'accidental negligence' as in such a case negligence had to be con-sidered by charges laid before a criminal court and therefore 'felonious': 'Undoubtedly there was no felonious intent, and probably no man in this court is more sorry for what has occurred to this fellow Rice; but at the same time, if he was appointed to take charge of those signals, and failed to do so through loss of memory or illness, he would have been receiving the railway company's money as their servant, and if he did not fulfil all the duties necessary in that employment it would be felonious neglect'.

After further debate, in which the jury declined the opportunity to retire and once again review all the evidence, the solicitor representing George Rice tried in vain to convince the Coroner that the jury's intention was to clear his client by simply returning a verdict equivalent to 'acci-dental death'. Dr Cordwent confirmed that the verdict as it stood would exonerate his client from all responsibility for the accident. The foreman of the jury announced 'We have no objection to a verdict of "accidental death "', which was greeted by a chorus of disapproval from his fellow jurors who made it clear that they did not regard Rice as totally blameless in the affair. At length, a juror rose and explained their position to the Coroner: 'It would save a good deal of misapprehension if I explained that the jury fully expected Rice would be committed for manslaughter. They merely wished to put this verdict in as extenuating a form as possi-ble'. Dr Cordwent had previously directed that 'manslaughter is a very ugly word' therefore, after further discussion it was finally agreed to add a rider to the jury's original verdict: 'We consider that the collision on the Great Western Railway, which caused the death of ten persons at Norton

MURDER & MYSTERY ON THE GWR

Fitzwarren arose through George Rice forgetting that he had, owing to the sidings being full, placed a down goods train on the main up line, and allowing it to remain there after putting the signals at "line clear" for the coming special up train. We further consider that, had there been sufficient siding accommodation between Taunton and Norton, the accident would not have occurred ... and that the said George Rice did negligently cause the death of several persons by the conditions above stated'.

Dr Cordwent then addressed George Rice: 'Strong sympathy has been expressed in your favour, but the law has certain rigid rules, and these rules must be followed. It is an unfortunate thing that, when you were in bad health, you still remained in an office of which you now appear to have been incapable, and as a result of which several persons have lost their lives. We have no objection to admit you to bail, but you will have to appear in another Court to answer for this occurrence'.

Subsequently, a magistrates hearing committed George Rice to face charges of manslaughter and he was brought to trail at Taunton before Mr Justice Grantham on Saturday 22 November.

Defence lawyer Charles Matthews insisted that his client's employer was responsible for allowing the dangerous practice of shunting trains on to main lines instead of branch lines or sidings. The staff on the goods train had also contributed to the accident in two ways; the driver had removed a red light from the front of the engine and the guard had neglected to go to the signal box.

In summing up, his Lordship pointed out that the case was a most serious one, not only as affecting the accused, but also as affecting the welfare of many travellers by rail. However much the jury might sympathise with the prisoner, they must not shrink from their responsibility if they believed he was guilty of negligence. There was no doubt that the actions of the driver and the guard of the goods train did nothing to divert a tragedy, but this did not exonerate the accused. If they considered his admitted lapse of memory a crime they must find him culpable.

After an hour's deliberation, the jury of fourteen men delivered a verdict of 'Not Guilty' and the foreman commented that they considered that 'a man of the prisoner's age should not be working alone in a signal box at night'.

Thus concluded a dramatic chapter in the annals of railway disasters in which the horrific opening episode had been eloquently put into context by a correspondent of the *Times*: 'The pitch darkness of the night, the flickering lights of lanterns, the fiery glow of the scattered embers of the engine furnaces, the dull red glare of the signal lamps, and the steady fall of the cold rain, all combined to make up a scene of terror and confusion perhaps unsurpassed in the railway history of England'.

RAILWAY MANIA
Young Isambard (named after eminent engineer): 'I say Dizzy, what's railway mania?'
Young Disraeli (named after prominent politician): 'Dunno Issy, but
they're going loco in the City'

Railway Mania Chairmen & Loco Engineers

In the early years of Queen Victoria's reign, there was a rush of investors willing to buy shares in railroads hoping to make their fortunes in the rapidly expanding market. Even Brunel once noted in his journal, 'I have made more [money] by my Great Western shares than by all my professional work'. However, many other railroad companies failed to have their schemes accepted by Parliament, resulting in huge losses for their shareholders. These periods of frenetic speculation were dubbed 'Railway Mania' – a term which might also apply to two successful chairmen of the GWR who were afflicted by 'temporary insanity'. After contributing so much in public life they both went 'off the rails' and chose to die by their own hand.

Four days before his untimely death, wealthy London merchant William Unwin Sims, admitted to his personal physician that he had 'too many irons in the fire'. He had interests in companies involved in insurance, overseas trading, iron and steel. In addition he was a director of the Bank of England and had been appointed chairman of the GWR in 1837. During his tenure, he had overseen the advent of the company's first train service from Paddington to Maidenhead in June 1838 and in January 1839 had averted a crisis when growing criticism of the broad gauge principle led Brunel to offer his resignation.

In mid-November 1839, Sims visited a solicitor and complained about being 'worn out' by business. He arranged to have a legal document drawn up giving full powers for his brother Frederick to manage his affairs while he went abroad to rest for a period of several months with another brother Henry who was planning a trip to Spain. A third brother Charles was in India and William had bought him a large 'horse pistol' to protect him on his travels. However, the gift had been turned down as unsuitable and was kept in a case in the drawing room of William's lodgings in Maddox Street, then part of Regent Street in central London. Sims, a single man aged forty-three, had lived at this address for eleven years and on Wednesday 15 November 1839, he returned home at 10.30pm and was handed a nightlight by his landlady Miss Ann Gressier. Although Sims never addressed her 'except when he desired something' she noticed that he appeared 'depressed in spirits' and stood in the hall for some time before climbing the stairs to his rooms. Next morning Sims's valet William Brent arrived at the house shortly before 8am and prepared his master's clothes for the day then left without seeing his employer who was 'a gentleman that seldom exchanged words with his servant'. Shortly after 9am, a relative of Sims, Mrs Hosen, called on him and Ann Gressier became concerned when she knocked on his bedroom door and received no answer. She sent for his manservant Brent who knowing that his master was a creature of habit, immediately came to the conclusion that Sims must be dead. His fears were realised when he entered the bedroom and drew back the bed curtains to be faced with a ghastly sight. The butchered remains of William Unwin Sims were laying on the bed; in his right hand was clenched his brother's pistol, 'the contents of which had evidently been discharged into the deceased's mouth, as the shattered remnant of his head was reclining on the pillow'.

A doctor was summoned and found that the ball had entered the mouth and passed through the brain before lodging in the back of the skull. In the medic's opinion Sims had been dead from four to six hours and it was likely that the gun was fired while in a sitting position before he fell backwards on to the pillow 'in the agonies of death'.

The news was greeted with incredulity by the GWR board. The company secretary, George Gibbs, who was one of the last people to see Sims alive, noted in his diary: 'We were all dreadfully shocked with this most unexpected tragedy, as there was nothing in his manner or conduct or circumstances to create the slightest suspicion of such an event'.

On Sunday evening, the inquest was held at the Coach and Horses public house in Maddox Street. Dr Gordon, who had been the Sims's family physician for twenty years was called to give evidence and expressed an opinion that the deceased was 'the very last man he should have thought would have committed suicide'. However, William Unwin Sims had visited him the previous Monday and been anxious about a 'beloved sister' who had recently been diagnosed as having developed a mental illness resulting in a 'deprivation of intellect'. The doctor agreed with a solicitor representing the Sims family, that the sudden death 'could not have taken place in any other way' than a 'paroxysm of insanity'. It was also revealed that the deceased had recently insured his own life for £20,000, which was an unusually large amount for a single man who had amassed a considerable personal fortune. The beneficiaries of Sims's estate were his siblings and although one of his brothers was at the inquest, the family solicitor suggested that it would be insensitive to call him to give evidence. When one of the jurors expressed a wish to examine the brother he was howled down by fellow jurors with cries of 'No, No'. The Coroner, Mr Higgs agreed and summed up: 'I think gentlemen, the evidence of Dr Gordon and Miss Gressier leaves scarcely any doubt of the deceased's insanity at the time he destroyed himself. You have heard that a paroxysm of insanity frequently comes on, and cannot be accounted for from the previous habits of a party. I knew myself a gentleman who was a collector to a musical society, and he had his pocket picked of some money belonging to the funds of the society. He told the society of his loss, and they believed it; but the circumstances so preyed upon the mind of the gentleman, that in a paroxysm of rage he stabbed himself; and upon his recovering from the wound he declared that he had no realisation whatever of having inflicted the injury'.

Having shared this personal knowledge with the jury, the Coroner asked them if they wished to have the public cleared from the room while they considered their verdict. The foreman rose and declared this was not necessary: 'I believe all my brother jurors are satisfied that it was a case of insanity'. The same member who had objected earlier protested that he could not agree with such a verdict. Clearly irritated the Coroner retorted: 'Well, gentleman, there are fifteen of you, and if twelve agree to a verdict that will be sufficient'. Without further ado it was pronounced by a majority of fourteen to one that William Unwin Sims had 'destroyed himself whilst labouring under a fit of temporary insanity'.

The GWR's successor to William Unwin Sims was Charles Russell. Descended from the aristocratic Bedford family, Charles was the second son of Sir Henry Russell, 1st Baronet of Swallowfield Park, near Reading, whose brother Lord John Russell became Prime Minister in 1846. As MP for Reading, Charles Russell served as Chairman of the committee that steered the Great Western Railway Act through Parliament in 1835.

A few months after taking office as Chairman of the GWR, Charles Russell received the devastating news that his septuagenarian great-uncle Lord William Russell had been murdered at his London home. On the morning of 6 May 1840, housemaid Susan Mancer discovered that the ground floor rooms of the residence in Park Lane had been ransacked. Fearing a robbery, she summoned the valet Francois Courvoisier and together they went to their master's bedchamber to inform him of the break-in. When the shutters were drawn the light revealed the blood-soaked body of Lord Russell lying on the bed with his throat cut.

The police were called to investigate and immediately came to the conclusion that the robbery had been staged to cover-up an inside job. Missing gold and silver articles were quickly found wrapped in a parcel inside the house and it seemed most unlikely that a thief would have left his plunder behind. The discovery of money and more gold articles secreted in the valet's pantry led to the arrest of Courvoisier who denied any involvement in the crime. Overwhelming proof was found when an inventory of the house revealed several missing items of silverware. Descriptions were circulated on handbills to silversmiths and pawnbrokers leading to their recovery that further incriminated the Swiss-born culprit. It transpired that Lord Russell had demanded Courvoisier's resignation when he discovered that his personal servant had been disposing of the family silver. Rather than face the disgrace of losing his position in the household, Courvoisier killed his employer hoping to conceal the scandal. For his heinous crime the treacherous valet was executed at Newgate Prison on 6 July 1840. A confession was issued from the condemned cell: 'After I had warmed his Lordship's bed; I went downstairs and waited about an hour, during which time I placed the various articles as they were found by the police. I afterwards went to the dining room, and took one of the knives from the sideboard. I then entered his bedroom and found him asleep. I went to the side of the bed, and drew the knife across his throat. He appeared to die instantly'.

Charles Russell was also shocked by the sudden death of his younger brother the Reverend William Whitworth Russell, who combined his incumbency of Chiddingley Church, East Sussex with the chaplainry of

Charles Russell

Millbank Prison. The country vicar was also an Inspector of HM Prisons for London and the Home Counties and campaigned tirelessly for penal reform. On Monday 2 August 1847, the clergyman was attending to his duties at Millbank Prison when he complained that he was feeling unwell and 'unfit for prison business'. At 4pm he asked for a glass of water, which he drank in the prison secretary's office before going to the board-room. Thirty minutes later, the report of muffled firearms was heard, but prison officials assumed the noise was a starting pistol at the Thames Regatta being held on the nearby river. Soon afterwards the truth dawned when the prison governor, Mr Watson, entered the passage between the boardroom and the armoury and discovered the body of Whitworth Russell spread-eagled on the floor. Laying on his back in a pool of blood, there was a pocket pistol by his side that had been discharged into the roof of the mouth; the ball having penetrated the brain and shattered the skull. Letters found on the corpse – addressed to the governor and an offi-cial at the Home Office – begged that news of his action should be sup-pressed until members of his family had been notified of his death. It transpired that earlier that afternoon the churchman had bought a pair of pistols in Regent Street, having spent the previous weekend in bed. Beset with financial worries through unwise investments in railway shares which did not perform well enough to fund the extravagant lifestyle of his socialite daughter Fanny, he lapsed into a severe depression and ended his life at the age of fifty-one.

The day following the catastrophic incident, an inquest was held in the boardroom of Millbank Prison. The Coroner, Mr Bedford, summed up for the jury who immediately reached a verdict that 'Deceased destroyed himself, being at the time of unsound mind'.

Horribly, Charles Russell's life was to end in similar fashion to that of his brother. Nine months after his long association with the GWR ended, when he retired through ill health in his seventieth year, he was found dying by his valet Robert Howard on 15 May 1856. Shortly before 7am the servant entered the bedroom and found the unconscious figure of his master lying on the bed. Russell was breathing hard and bleeding heavily from the nose and mouth. By his side were two pistols; one of the weapons had evidently misfired, while the other had found its target. A surgeon, Mr M'Oscar was soon in attendance; upon examining the patient's mouth he saw a large fissure in the centre of the palate where the ball had entered before lodging in the brain. The injuries had been inflicted up to two hours previously, though the valet and the house-keeper had not heard the shot. Although the wound was fatal, death was far from instantaneous and Russell's life lingered for several hours before his suffering mercifully ended at 2pm. It appeared that Russell had stood at the side of his bed in his dressing gown armed with a loaded pistol in each hand. Unnervingly, when he pulled the trigger of the pistol in his right hand, the bullet remained in the barrel. Undeterred, he then placed the pistol in his left hand to his mouth, which fired successfully before the recoil caused him to fall backwards onto the bed where he lapsed into unconsciousness.

Mr Bedford, the Coroner for Westminster who had earlier officiated at the inquest of the Reverend Whitworth Russell, heard from Charles Russell's personal physician Dr Morton that the deceased had been suffering from a chest illness which had induced a state of depression leading to mental derangement. The jury found that the deceased had perished during a bout of 'Temporary insanity'.

The disgrace brought on the family name, by what was viewed as the dishonourable deaths of Whitworth and Charles Russell, was redressed by the suicidal bravery of their nephew Brevet Major Sir Charles Russell. During the Crimean War the gallant officer 'performed prodigies of valour' against overwhelming odds at the Battle of Inkerman and was one of the first recipients of the Victoria Cross bestowed by the monarch in 1857. Five years earlier his Uncle Charles was awarded an honour of his own by the GWR in recognition of his fine service laying the foundations of the company's success. The tribute was announced in the *Railway Times*, 10 January 1852:

Great Western. – At a meeting of the officers and servants of this Company, held last week at the Swindon Station, Mr. Gooch in the Chair, it was stated that 1,900 officers, clerks, and servants in the employment of the Company had united in subscribing £420 for the purpose of obtaining a full-length portrait of Mr. C. Russell, the Chairman of the Company, to be placed in the Board Room of the Paddington Station, as a testimonial of their grateful esteem for the high principles of honour, impartiality, and undeviating kindness he has ever displayed towards them; and also to record their sense of the eminent services rendered by him to the Company, over which he has so long and efficiently presided.

Artist Francis Grant R.A. produced a full-length likeness and thereafter whenever a company employee was summoned to the boardroom, either as culprit or witness in an inquiry, it was commonly referred to by the staff as 'Going to see the picture'. At the unveiling Charles Russell expressed his admiration for the workforce: 'I never have lost and I never can lose any opportunity of expressing my conviction that no public body was ever more ably, zealously, and honourably served than the Great Western'.

Another distinguished chairman of the GWR was Daniel Gooch who in 1837 had begun a long association with the company as Superintendent Locomotive Engineer. When he resigned to take over as chairman in 1864, the locomotive post went to Joseph Armstrong who for the next thirteen years was overlord of the works at Swindon before he died suddenly whilst on holiday in 1877. Joseph Armstrong left a dynasty of fine locomotive engineers as two of his sons and a grandson followed in his footsteps. The brightest prospect was his fourth son and namesake Joseph, known as 'Young Joe'. In 1876, the GWR took the logical step of taking over the running of the various companies in which they already had a financial interest, namely the West Cornwall, the Bristol & Exeter and the South Devon railways. From the latter, the amalgamation led to the transfer of a talented young engineer from Newton Abbot to Swindon. His name was George Jackson Churchward who served the final year of his apprenticeship alongside 'Young Joe' and the pair became firm friends. A few years after the death of Joe's father, the new supremo William Dean set the two youngsters a task to develop an effective braking system. Up to this time all that had been provided to stop a train was a primitive handbrake on the engine and guards van, which had proved inadequate and dangerous. Armstrong and Dean developed the concept of 'continuous' brakes along the length of the train operated by air and vacuum brakes that were applied automatically if carriages became separated in an accident.

'Young Joe' Armstrong was seen as the obvious successor to William Dean. Rising to Assistant Divisional Locomotive Superintendent at

Swindon: 'a proud tradition of railway engineering'

Swindon, he was promoted again in 1885 when he moved to Wolverhampton as works manager under his uncle George Armstrong. Although a bright future seemed assured, Joe Armstrong's life was dogged by ill health. At the end of his apprenticeship he went on a sea voyage to South Africa where his recuperation was cut short by the news of his father's death. Ten years later during Christmas 1887, Joe was feeling unwell suffering from neuralgia and a chest ailment. Due to return to work on New Year's Day, he called into the locomotive department on the evening before and wished his men 'Happy New Year'. Shortly after midnight he left the works to walk home along the line. At 12.30am, he was hit and killed by a shunting goods engine. As the train ran over him, his decapitated body was spotted lying on the line by the shocked guard. When investigations began it soon became obvious that the occurrence was no accident. The deceased had written to a friend stating that death was the only solution to his mounting debt problems and that by the time the letter was read he would in all probability have been 'run over'. Each of his numerous creditors had also been sent cheques giving them the name of his insurance company where they could apply for payment. At the inquest, the jury returned a verdict of 'suicide while temporary insane'.

Years later, his friend George Churchward generously acknowledged that had he lived, 'Young Joe' would doubtless have become Locomotive Superintendent of the GWR. However, Churchward proved more than able to fill the post. The son of a country squire born on 31 January 1857 in the South Devon village of Stoke Gabriel, he would have witnessed the opening of the Dartmouth to Kingswear Railway in August 1864 which had been planned by Brunel before his death. Churchward later attended a Grammar School at nearby Totnes on the Newton Abbot to Plymouth line and growing up in the close proximity to the broad gauge railway stimulated an interest in steam locomotives. The Churchward family had been farming stock since the end of the fifteenth century, yet, remarkably, four of Churchward's cousins also left the rural idyll of Stoke Gabriel to pursue successful careers as veritable railway missionaries: George Dundas Churchward built the Tientsin-Tangshan railway in China; William Patrick Churchward was honoured by the Italian government for his contribution to their rail network; Alaric Watts Churchward was appointed Paris agent for the London, Chatham & Dover Railway; Joseph Churchward was awarded the mail contract linking the railways between Dover and Calais before becoming MP for Dover. However, the genius of the family was undoubtedly George Jackson Churchward who at the age of sixteen became a probationer engineer at the South Devon Railway's locomotive works at Newton Abbot. Three years later he moved to the

Stoke Gabriel: the birthplace of Churchward

drawing office at Swindon and rose steadily through the ranks. Churchward proved his worth in a variety of positions of increasing responsibility before he became chief assistant to the ailing William Dean in 1897 and officially succeeded him as Locomotive Superintendent when his mentor bowed out through ill health in 1902. During his period in charge Churchward streamlined production and maintenance with a standardised range of engines utilising interchangeable components. Under his supervision boiler efficiency was vastly improved and locomotive design was advanced by adapting the best facets of Continental and American engineering practice that were incorporated in his famous 'Star' and 'Saint' class steam engines. Churchward also experimented by building a gigantic American style Pacific loco called *The Great Bear*. Due to its weight and size it was restricted to travelling on the line between Bristol and London where it was often utilised to carry goods to and from Fry's chocolate factory at Bristol. In 1920 the 'Cocoa Train', as it was dubbed, became the target of a group of schoolboys standing on a bridge and attempting to drop stones down the chimney as the train passed below. One of the culprits apprehended and cautioned was the son of Churchward's second cousin Brigadier-General Paul Churchward. The prankster Paul junior, known as 'Bob' to his family and friends, grew up to become an intrepid jungle explorer mapping the mysterious Rio das Morentes region of Brazil while leading an unsuccessful search for missing explorer Percy Fawcett, whom it was later assumed had fallen into the clutches of a tribe of cannibals on the Amazon.

The Churchward family motto: 'Swift as the bird flies' took on a new dimension when GWR locomotives started breaking speed records. It must have been a proud moment for Churchward in March 1902, when royalty sped along the banks of the River Dart passing his ancestral home at Stoke Gabriel on a record-breaking journey. The train carried King Edward VII and Queen Alexandra on their way to lay the foundation stone for the new Britannia Royal Naval College at Dartmouth. Appropriately drawn by the locomotive *Britannia*, it set a non-stop record by covering the 229 miles from London via Bristol to Kingswear in 4 hours 23 minutes. A year later, when the Duke of Cornwall, the future King George V, was on his way to visit the Duchy, one of Churchward's newest creations the *City of Bath* ran non-stop from London to Plymouth in record time completing the journey of just over 245 miles in 3hrs 53 minutes at an average speed of 63.4 mph.

'Records crowd upon records in this remarkable year of railway history' commented journalist Charles Rous-Marten in the *Railway Magazine*, June 1904. Following the success of the royal trains, times tumbled when the GWR introduced a non-stop two-way service between Paddington and Plymouth, the longest run in the world by regular trains. This was achieved by the introduction of corridor trains and onboard toilets for the comfort of passengers plus a 'slip coach' system that released mail carriages at points along the line without the necessity of stopping. Fast runs became important, as there was fierce competition from the GWR's rivals, the London & South Western Railway. In effect the two companies were racing each other to secure mail contracts. The GWR's Ocean Mail express met liners docking at Millbay Docks,

The locomotive Britannia *at* Kingswear

Plymouth and sped passengers and cargo to the Capital. It was during one of these journeys in May 1904 that Churchward's *City of Truro* became the first locomotive to travel at a speed in access of 100mph. The GWR had adopted a popular slogan – 'The Line that put the 'ees' in spEEd', although the company played down talk of maximum speeds and sought publicity for their express services by showing increases in average speeds and reductions in journey times. They were wary of public reaction as letters to the press revealed that many passengers were clearly concerned by the safety aspect of travelling at 'fearful speeds'. Therefore, Charles Rous-Marten, a respected authority on locomotive performances who timed the first 100mph run was denied permission to publish the top speed achieved, although avid readers of his features were tantalised with a description of 'a hurricane descent' made down Wellington Bank by the *City of Truro* in an article which appeared under the banner headline 'The Great Western Railway's Record of Records' When continually pressed for more detailed information by readers, Rous-Marten could contain himself no longer and eventually revealed his secret confirming that during the record run the *City of Truro* achieved the 'unprecedented rate of 102.3mph'. The railway journalist's exciting disclosure appeared in the May 1908 edition of *Railway Magazine,* although sadly the author never lived to witness the reaction. Following a bout of influenza he collapsed and died after suffering a massive heart attack on 20 April – Easter Monday. Aged sixty-four he had written his last 'exclusive'.

The GWR adopted the slogan – 'The Line that put the 'ees' in spEEd'

In the same month of Rous-Marten's sudden demise, Churchward was rocked by the suicide of an employee for which he bore some responsibility. Possibly due to his upbringing as the son of a country squire, Churchward had an abrupt manner with underlings and was considered stern and autocratic; nevertheless he was fair-minded and well liked by the workforce who referred to him affectionately as the 'Old Man'. However, his role as Locomotive Superintendent also involved dealing with personnel matters for which he was rather less well qualified. Petty theft was common amongst staff who considered it a 'perk of the job'. Those apprehended were usually prosecuted and dealt with by the courts then dismissed by the company if found guilty. One case went disastrously wrong when Churchward dealt summarily with a transgressor, a sixty-nine year old engine driver who was caught stealing a small amount of coal from a tender. Nearly twenty years earlier the old driver had suffered a nervous breakdown when he was transferred against his wishes from Swindon to Bristol. After receiving treatment in an asylum he was allowed to return to work in a reduced capacity turning round locomotives in the engine yard. When the theft of coal was brought to Churchward's attention, he reduced the old man's pay by 40% and stipulated that he should retire at the end of the year. Next day, the body of the drowned loco driver was found floating in the canal.

Churchward's life was also fated to end in tragic circumstances and in a similar way to that of his friend Joe Armstrong. Following an early retirement in 1921, the 'Old Man' spent a lot of time fishing with a rod that had been presented to him by the workforce. Unmarried, he was cared for by a housekeeper and a chauffeur-valet, while he continued to live in his company residence Newburn House near the Swindon works. He still took a keen interest in company matters and at 10.20 on the morning of 19 December 1933, he told his valet that he was concerned about the condition of the track on the main line and was going to take a look at it. As he passed through a gate with private access to the line, he ignored a warning from his gardener that conditions were too dangerous to venture out on the track. Visibility was poor owing to thick fog, and now aged seventy-six, Churchward's eyesight was fading and had been treated for glaucoma. In addition to the elderly man's eyesight problem his hearing was also impaired and he neither saw nor heard the Paddington to Fishguard Express, *George Jackson Churchward*

131

which was running late. In consequence, as he stooped over the line to inspect the sleepers he was struck on the head by the front buffer of the locomotive *Berkeley Castle*. Churchward was killed instantly, although no one on the train was aware of the incident as it hurtled past. Soon afterwards, the lifeless body was found lying prostrate alongside the line by a ganger. An inquest determined the cause as 'accidental death' and the civic funeral that followed brought Swindon to a standstill as crowds lined the route of the cortege. In his address to the mourners, the Bishop of Barking commented on the supreme irony of 'the great locomotive engineer killed by one of his own creations'. Churchward's attributes as an engineer and a man were summed up admirably in an obituary that appeared in the *Times:*

> To the public the Churchward era at Swindon was synonymous with speed and fine locomotive performance; to engineers it was charged with the interest that comes with continuous mechanical development; and to Churchward's staff and the men at the works that he controlled so ably it meant loyalty, respect, and affection for the fine character that inspired these feelings.

Guidelines laid down by Churchward dictated the design concepts of all steam locos until steam power was phased out in favour of diesel engines on what remained of the railroads after the fall of the 'Beeching Axe' in the 1960's. Sir Nigel Gresley, who in the 1930's designed the world's fastest steam locomotive the *Mallard*, once paid this tribute to Churchward: 'Locomotive engineers owe more to his ingenuity, inventiveness and foresight than to any other engineer'.

Unforgivably, in 1905, Churchward ordered the destruction of the last remaining broad gauge engines *North Star* and *Lord of the Isles* preserved at the Swindon works, the reason given being 'these engines are occupying valuable space in our shops'. The forward thinking Churchward evidently had no sentiment for railway heritage, although he could never have envisaged the end of a proud tradition of railway engineering in Swindon. Founded by Brunel and Gooch in 1842, the GWR works which had been an integral part of the renowned 'railway town' for 150 years, were demolished in the 1990's. The 240-acre site was developed into a huge housing, leisure, shopping and industrial complex. This community now known as 'Churchward' also commemorates the railway engineer's wider role in the history of Swindon. When the New Swindon Urban District Council was established in 1894, Churchward was elected a member and became chairman in 1897. With the incorporation of old and new towns in 1900 he became the borough's first mayor and had the distinction of becoming the first Freeman of the Borough in 1921. During the First World War, the railway works was devoted largely to the production of munitions under Churchward's direction and his contribution to the war effort was recognised with the award of the CBE in 1918.

An equally fitting tribute to Churchward's memory was the naming of a locomotive in his honour in 1948. A year earlier, the railroads had been nationalised by the post-war government and until the industry reverted to privatisation half a century later, the revered name of the GWR was consigned to history. Indeed, over the passage of time and a plethora of ill-conceived legislation, bungling politicians have often been accused of committing the worst 'Acts' of 'Murder & Mystery on the Great Western Railway'.

Bibliography & Sources

General Sources on the History of the Great Western Railway

Awdry, Christopher. *Brunel's Broad Gauge Railway*, Oxford, Oxford Publishing Co., 1992

MacDermot, E.T. *History of the Great Western Railway*, Vol. I 1833-1863, London, Great Western Railway Company, 1927

MacDermot, E.T. *History of the Great Western Railway*, Vol. 2 1863-1921, London, Great Western Railway Company, 1931

Body, Geoffrey. *Western Handbook, A Digest of GWR and WR Data*, Weston-super-Mare, British Rail (Western) in association with Avon-AngliA Publications & Services, 1985

Williams, Archibald. *Brunel And After: The Romance of the Great Western Railway*, London, The Great Western Railway, 1925

The Railway Magazine, The Great Western Issue, IPC Country & Leisure Media, December 2005

Website sources:

British Transport Police: www.bt.police.co.uk

The Great Western Archive: www.greatwestern.org.uk

THE ACCIDENT PRONE LIFE OF ISAMBARD KINGDOM BRUNEL

Gooch, Daniel Sir, Bart. *Diaries of Sir Daniel Gooch*, London. Kegan Paul & Co. 1892

Griffiths, Denis. *Locomotive Engineers of the GWR*, Wellingborough, Northants. Patrick Stephens Ltd., 1987

Kay, Peter. *Rails Along the Sea Wall*, Sheffield. Platform 5 Publishing Ltd., 1990

Matthew, HCG. and Harris, Brian (eds) *Oxford Dictionary of National Biography*, Oxford. Oxford University Press 2004

Rolt, L.T.C. *Isambard Kingdom Brunel,* London. Longmans, Green & Co Ltd., 1953

Contemporary Journals: *Bristol Mirror, Illustrated London News, Plymouth Times, The Times, Torquay Chronicle and General Directory, Woolmer's Exeter and Plymouth Gazette*

THE CORNISH VIADUCT TRAGEDIES

Bennett Alan. *The Great Western Railway in West Cornwall*, Southampton, Kingfisher Railway Productions, 1988

Binding, John. *Brunel's Cornish Viaducts*, Penryn, Pendragon Books, 1993

Clinker, C.R. *The Railways of Cornwall 1809-1963*, Dawlish. David & Charles, 1963

Rolt, L.T.C. *Isambard Kingdom Brunel*, London. Longmans, Green & Co Ltd., 1953

Contemporary Journals: *Illustrated London News, Plymouth Journal, The Times, West Briton & Cornwall Advertiser, Western Daily Mercury, Western Morning News*

THE KILLER KWAKER

Head, Francis Bond, Sir, Bart. *Stokers and Pokers*, London, John Murray, 1849

Williams, Archibald. *Brunel and After: The Romance of the Great Western Railway*, London, The Great Western Railway,1925

Contemporary Journals: *The Globe, Illustrated London News, The Sun, Sydney Gazette, The Times, Windsor and Eton Express*

THE GREAT WESTERN TRAIN ROBBERY &
THE BERMONDSEY MURDER

Alpert, Michael. *London 1849*, Harlow, Pearson Education Ltd., 2004

Borowitz, Albert. *The Bermondsey Horror*, London, Robson Books, 1988

Huish, Robert. *The Progress of Crime or the Authentic Memoirs of Maria Manning*, London, 1849

Matthew, HCG. and Harris, Brian (eds) *Oxford Dictionary of National Biography*, Oxford. Oxford University Press, 2004

Contemporary Journals: *Exeter Gazette, Illustrated London News, Taunton Courier, Times, Trewman's Exeter Flying Post*

THE MEN THEY DID NOT HANG

Holgate, Mike. *Secret of the Babbacombe Murder*, Newton Abbot, Peninsula Press 1995

Holgate, Mike. Waugh, Ian. *The Man They Could Not Hang*, Stroud, Sutton Publishing Ltd., 2005

Lee, John. *The Man They Could Not Hang*, London, C. Arthur Pearson, 1908

The Great Western Illustrated Railway Guide, London, c1875

Contemporary Journals: *East & South Devon Advertiser, News of the World, The Times, Torquay Directory & South Devon Journal, Torquay Times & South Devon Advertiser, West London Observer*

GREAT BLIZZARDS AND GREAT ESCAPES

The Blizzard in the West, London, Simpkin, Marshall, Hamilton, Kent & Co., 1891

Rhodes, A.J. *Dartmoor Prison*, London, John Lane The Bodley Head Ltd., 1933

Thomson, Basil, *The Story of Dartmoor Prison*, London, William Heinemann, 1907

Barber, Chips. *Railways on and around Dartmoor*, Exeter, Obelisk Publications, 1997

Contemporary Journals: *Illustrated London News, The Times, Torquay Times & South Devon Advertiser, Western Daily Mercury, Western Morning News*

BIZARRE RAILWAY SUICIDES

Pike, John. *Iron Horse to the Sea*, Bradford on Avon, Ex Libris Press, 1987

Bird, Sheila. *Cornish Tales of Mystery & Murder*, Newbury, Berkshire, Countryside Books, 2002

Contemporary Journals: *Berkshire Chronicle, Daily News, Illustrated Police News, Pall Mall Gazette, Punch, Reading Mercury, The Times, Torquay Directory & South Devon Journal, West Briton & Cornwall Advertiser, Western Morning News*

THE NORTON FITZWARREN TRAIN DISASTERS

Kingdom, A.R. *The Railway Accident at Norton Fitzwarren, 1940*, Newton Abbot, Ark Publications (Railways), 2005

Vaughan, Adrian. *Grime and Glory*, Gloucester, Alan Sutton Publishing, 1985

Contemporary Journals: *Illustrated London News, Somerset County Herald, The Times, Western Morning News*

RAILWAY MANIA CHAIRMEN & LOCO ENGINEERS

Griffiths, Denis. *Locomotive Engineers of the GWR*, Wellingborough, Northants. Patrick Stephens Ltd., 1987

Matthew, HCG. and Harris, Brian (eds) *Oxford Dictionary of National Biography*, Oxford. Oxford University Press, 2004

Rogers, HCB, Colonel. *G.J. Churchward A Locomotive Biography*, London, George Allen & Unwin Ltd., 1975

Contemporary Journals: *Great Western Railway Magazine, Railway Magazine, Railway Times, The Times*